exercises that
create cooperation
(power shared)

cf.
those that don't

UNIVERSITY ASSOCIATES
Publishers and Consultants

SERIES IN HUMAN RELATIONS TRAINING

A Handbook of Structured Experiences for Human Relations Training

Volume V

Edited by

J. WILLIAM PFEIFFER, Ph.D.
Human Relations Consultant
La Jolla, California

JOHN E. JONES, Ph.D.
Human Relations Consultant
La Jolla, California

UNIVERSITY ASSOCIATES
Publishers and Consultants
7596 Eads Avenue
La Jolla, California 92037

PREFACE

The publication of this fifth volume of *A Handbook of Structured Experiences for Human Relations Training* reaffirms our intention to serve as a clearinghouse for new ideas and new approaches developed by group facilitators in human relations training. We are pleased that readers continue to adapt, restructure, and expand structured experiences to suit their own particular purposes. We encourage the extension of these materials, and we continue to be interested in receiving structured experiences or instruments that users of our publications have developed.

Volume V, we think, demonstrates the strength and value of the materials we have received. The structured experiences in this volume are convenient, useful, and adaptable to a variety of settings.

We also are gratified that the number of people who use our structured experiences continues to grow every year. The fact that our materials are now published in several foreign languages and distributed in many countries indicates the increasing interest in this experiential technology.

Since human relations training materials are generally the result of shared ideas, alterations, and adaptations, it is consistently difficult to ascertain the source or sources of any particular experience or instrument. However, in accordance with our previously stated policy, we have made a conscientious effort to identify accurately the sources of the activities in this volume.

As with our previous *Handbooks* and the *Annuals,* users should feel free to duplicate and/or modify the forms, charts, descriptions, instruments, and activities for use in education/training designs. However, *systematic or large-scale reproduction or distribution—or inclusion of items in publications for sale—may be done only with prior written permission.*

Volume V differs from previous *Handbooks* in that it is paperbound rather than spiral bound. We have initiated this new format in order to eliminate the difficulties in obtaining plastic binding materials and assembling the several components for spiral-bound books. Future editions of Volumes I through IV will also be published in this paper binding.

As with all publications in our Series in Human Relations Training, Volume V is directed toward the needs of facilitators. Our aim is to make useful and practical materials readily and widely available to practitioners in the human relations training field.

J. William Pfeiffer
John E. Jones

La Jolla, California
March, 1975

TABLE OF CONTENTS

―――

*See Introduction, p. 2, for explanation of numbering.

INTRODUCTION

The twenty-four structured experiences in this volume bring the number of these activities published in the Pfeiffer-Jones Series in Human Relations Training to 172. Our continuing emphasis on structured experiences is based on our increasing appreciation that this type of training design provides solid, transferable learning experiences that will produce generally predictable outcomes. Based on an experiential model, structured experiences are inductive rather than deductive, providing *direct* rather than vicarious learnings. Thus participants *discover* meaning for themselves and *validate* their own experience.

It is our belief that instruments (questionnaires, scales, and inventories) enhance and reinforce the learnings from structured experiences. Instruments also provide feedback to the facilitator on the appropriateness of the activity and the effectiveness of the presentation. In this volume, therefore, we have initiated a new feature. At the end of structured experiences, where applicable, "Suggested Instruments" lists additional instruments, other than those included in a particular structured experience, that may be used effectively with that structured experience. All sixteen of the suggested instruments appear in the Instrumentation sections of the 1972, 1973, 1974, and 1975 *Annuals* (four instruments in each volume). A list of these instruments is included at the back of this book. Instruments may be reproduced from the *Annuals* or ordered (in lots of twenty-five) from University Associates.

We also believe that any individual participating in a training event should expect his learning needs to be a prime concern of the facilitator. Thus, it is the responsibility of the facilitator to examine the specific needs and level of sophistication of the group and to choose a suitable structured experience. Adaptability and flexibility are therefore emphasized in the design of the structured experiences in this volume. The variations listed after each structured experience suggest possible alterations that a facilitator may wish to incorporate in order to make the experience more suitable to the particular design and to the needs of the participants. The expected norm in human relations training is innovation.

At the end of structured experiences in this volume are cross-references to similar structured experiences and lecturette sources. The number of each supplemental or complementary structured experience and the volume in which it appears are indicated. Lecturettes are listed by title and publication. Space for notes on each structured experience has been allowed for the convenience of the facilitator.

Our structured experiences are numbered consecutively throughout the series of *Handbooks* and *Annuals,* in order of publication of the volumes. Thus, the 172 structured experiences we have published are distributed among nine books—five *Handbooks* and four *Annuals.* The tabulated list on the next page specifies the numbers of the structured experiences to be found in each publication in the Pfeiffer-Jones Series in Human Relations Training.

Structured Experience	Publication
1 through 24	Volume I, *Handbook*
25 through 48	Volume II, *Handbook*
49 through 74	Volume III, *Handbook*
75 through 86	1972 *Annual*
87 through 100	1973 *Annual*
101 through 124	Volume IV, *Handbook*
125 through 136	1974 *Annual*
137 through 148	1975 *Annual*
149 through 172	Volume V, *Handbook*

As do the 1973, 1974, and 1975 *Annuals,* this volume contains a chart of all our published structured experiences according to category. This chart is found on the last two facing pages in this book. While this categorization is somewhat arbitrary, since each experience may be adapted for a variety of training purposes, we think that it will further aid the facilitator in selecting an appropriate activity. For easy location of a structured experience, the chart lists the title, number, volume, and page number of each experience.

Following all structured experiences in this volume is a list of contributors, with titles, addresses, and, where possible, telephone numbers, so that readers may contact individual authors directly.

In Volume V, as in other volumes of the *Handbook* and in the *Annuals,* the structured experiences are presented in order of the increasing understanding, skill, and experience required of the facilitator. The first structured experiences in the book require less expertise and generate less affect and data than do the last ones; consequently, the facilitator needs less skill and experience to use them effectively and responsibly. *Adequate processing is very important to the successful presentation of a structured experience.* Effective processing clarifies and reinforces learnings and allows participants to integrate their learning without undue stress. The facilitator's choice of structured experiences should, therefore, reflect not only the needs of the participants but also his own competence and experience.

We think that any facilitator concerned with these issues should be able to use these activities effectively to provide a valuable growth experience for participants in a human relations training design or workshop.

149. ENERGIZERS: GROUP STARTERS

Listed below are several brief activities that can be used at the beginning of a group session to prepare participants for the meeting. An "energizer" should be non-threatening, be fun, involve physical movement, stimulate breathing, and provide a shared experience. It is important for the facilitator to indicate that persons with physical impairments need not participate.

1. *The Scream.* Participants stand and close their eyes. They are told to breathe slowly and deeply. Then all members of the group breathe in unison. Continuing to breathe together, they reach up and then reach higher and higher. They are instructed to jump up and down together and then to scream as loudly as they can.

2. *Songs.* Participants stand on their tiptoes and walk about while they sing together "Tiptoe Through the Tulips." The song and movement are then changed to "Walking Through the Tulips," "Running Through the Tulips," and finally "Stomping Through the Tulips." (Other "activity" songs can be used, such as "Itsy Bitsy Spider," "Bunny Hop," and "Head and Shoulders, Knees and Toes.")

3. *Whoosh.* Participants stand, reach up, and breathe deeply in unison. Then they are told to bend forward quickly at the waist, dropping their arms as if they were going to touch their toes, while exhaling all the air in their lungs. This is repeated several times.

4. *Machine.* One person goes to the center of the room and acts out the repetitive motion and sound of a part of a machine. Others add parts to the machine, one by one, until the entire group is involved. Variation: Subgroups can be formed to devise or to act out (as in charades) machines that would manufacture concepts such as love, empathy, competition, etc.

5. *Computers.* Subgroups of four or five members each are designated to be "computers." They stand in semicircles, facing the facilitator. The facilitator inserts a "card" into one of the computers by saying the first word of a sentence ("Life . . . ," "Bosses . . . ," "Women . . . ," etc.). The "components" of the computer respond by creating the rest of the sentence, one word per person. The sentence is ended by one "component" saying "period," "question mark," or "exclamation point." The process is repeated with each of the other computers. Then the computers take turns asking questions of the other computers, e.g., "What is the meaning of life?" "Who will be the next President?"

Finally, the computers are linked together to build a sentence about the experience, with at least one word contributed by each component part.

6. *Nerf.* Participants stand in a circle and bounce a Nerf Ball (a soft, spongy ball distributed by Parker Brothers) or a balloon in the air as long as possible. Ground rules are as follows: (1) no person may hit the ball twice in a row; (2) the ball must not touch the floor; (3) before the ball can be hit randomly, it must be bounced at least once by each person around the complete circle; (4) the person who makes a bad pass must share something about himself with the group; and (5) the group makes binding decisions about "bad passes." (Allan G. Dorn.)

7. *Playground.* The facilitator announces that the group room is a playground. Participants act out swinging, climbing, sliding, etc.

8. *Elephant and Giraffe.* Participants stand in a circle, and one person volunteers to be "it." The volunteer stands in the center of the circle, points to one member, and says either "Elephant" or "Giraffe." The person pointed to and the participant on each side of him have to pantomime some part of the designated animal (nose, ears, neck, eyes, etc.) before the volunteer counts to three. If a person fails to respond in time, he becomes "it."

9. *Congo Line.* Participants line up, placing their hands on the waist of the person in front of them. Various rhythmic patterns can be used as the group moves about the room. "Serpent" variation: Members line up and hold hands; the person at the head of the line leads it through the room, coiling and winding like a snake.

10. *Hum.* The facilitator announces that on his signal the group will begin humming. Each participant hums any song that occurs to him. Members are encouraged to "interpret" their spontaneous choices of songs.

Similar Structured Experiences: *Vol. II:* Structured Experience 27; *Vol. IV:* **101;** *'74 Annual:* **125.**

Notes on the Use of "Energizers":

150. RIDDLES: INTERGROUP COMPETITION

Goals

I. To observe competitive behavior among groups.

II. To determine how a group interacts with other groups when it is dependent on them for the completion of its task.

Group Size

A minimum of twelve participants.

Time Required

Approximately one and one-half hours.

Materials

Four Riddles Envelope Sets, prepared according to the Directions for Making Riddles Envelope Sets.

Physical Setting

A large room in which four groups can meet concurrently in relative privacy.

Process

I. Prior to the session, the facilitator selects four participants to be observers. He gives them an overview of the activity and briefs them on what behaviors to observe. He also assigns to them the task of enforcing the rules. The observers are designated A, B, C, and D.

II. When participants are assembled, the facilitator forms four groups of nearly equal size. These groups are designated A, B, C, and D. The groups are seated in separate parts of the room. The observers begin their task, observer A observing group A, etc.

III. The facilitator announces that the task of each group will be to solve a riddle. To accomplish this task, each group must do two things: (a) obtain all the available information pertaining to the riddle, and (b) determine the correct solution. The winning group will be the one that assembles all its pieces and solves its riddle first. *The solution may not be submitted until all the pieces of the riddle are in the group's possession.* To obtain all clues for a particular riddle, a group must trade or barter with the other three groups for these clues. The conditions for exchanging clues are as follows:

1. Only one representative of a group may leave the group at any time.
2. Only one representative may negotiate with any group at one time.
3. A group's representative must change after each transaction with another group is completed.
4. A representative may not exchange (obtain or give) more than two clues during any transaction with another group.

IV. The groups are instructed to begin working on their tasks. (The facilitator may tell a group whether it has all the necessary pieces to solve its riddle. If all the pieces are present in the group, the facilitator may also indicate whether its solution is correct.)

V. When a winner is determined, the facilitator immediately stops the problem-solving phase. Groups are instructed to discuss their *process* and their feelings about the outcome. (Observers continue their task.)

VI. The facilitator and the group of four observers assemble in the center of the room. The facilitator leads a *discussion* (no speeches) of the intra- and intergroup phenomena.

VII. The facilitator opens up the discussion to include the entire group. He may solicit generalizations suggested by the experience as well as applications of these learnings to "back-home" situations.

VIII. The facilitator reads aloud each riddle and its correct solution. The solutions are:

Riddle 1. The missionaries and cannibals go back and forth across the river in the following series of diagrammed steps:

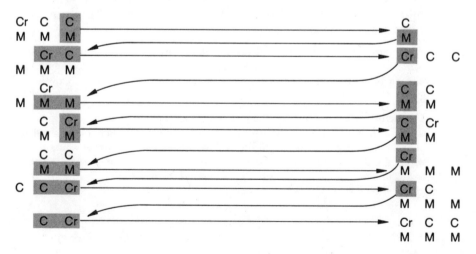

Riddle 2. Each man thought that his face looked like the other's.

Riddle 3. They tipped the barrel on the diagonal. If the liquid reached the lip and still covered the bottom, it was more than half full; if the bottom of the barrel showed, it was less than half full.

Riddle 4. He was a midget and could not reach any button above "8" on the elevator panel.

Variations

I. Other riddles can be used. There should be at least four sentences in each riddle.

II. The empty-chair design can be used in step VI (see *Volume III*, Structured Experience 51). Also, observers can report to groups privately before the total-group processing phase.

III. Two observers can be assigned to each group: one to observe only and one to enforce the rules.

IV. In step V, the problem solving can be allowed to continue until all riddles have been solved or a stalemate has been reached.

Similar Structured Experiences: *Vol. II:* Structured Experience **31**; *Vol. IV:* **102, 103.**
Lecturette Source: *'73 Annual:* "Win/Lose Situations."

Notes on the Use of "Riddles":

Submitted by Brian P. Holleran.

Structured Experience 150

DIRECTIONS FOR MAKING RIDDLES ENVELOPE SETS *

Each line of each riddle (including the letter and number) is typed on a separate 3″ × 5″ card. The letter and number are included in order to facilitate random distribution of information across the four groups and to enable the facilitator to determine whether a given group has all the information it needs to solve its riddle. All cards labeled "A" are placed in an envelope marked "A," all "B's" are placed in an envelope marked "B," and so on. (The numbers are sequential but not consecutive.)

Riddle 1

D 43	Three missionaries and three cannibals come to a river and desire to cross.
C 50	The boat will carry only two passengers.
A 57	All the missionaries can row, but only one of the cannibals has been trained to do this.
D 64	The trips must be arranged so that the cannibals will never outnumber the missionaries.
A 71	In other words, one missionary must never be in the company of two cannibals, or two missionaries with three cannibals.
B 78	They were able to get across, but how was it done?

Riddle 2

A 85	Two workmen were repairing a roof.
D 92	They fell through a large chimney and landed in a fireplace on the floor below.
C 99	Both men were unhurt.
D 106	They looked at each other, walked around the room, stretched their arms, and realized that they had sustained no injuries.
D 113	Without speaking a word or discussing their sudden fall, both men started back to their job.
C 120	It happened that one man's face was well smeared with soot from his passage through the chimney.
D 127	The other man's face, however, was absolutely clean.
A 134	Yet the man with the clean face went in and washed his face; the man with the dirty face went back to work without washing his face.
B 141	Can you explain, logically, why they did this?

Riddle 3

A 148   When Jimmy went to buy a barrel of cider from Farmer Brown, the farmer had only about one-half barrel of cider.

B 155   Jimmy looked into the barrel and thought it was less than one-half full, while the farmer thought it was more than one-half full.

C 162   They settled the matter quickly and accurately without using a measuring rod of any kind or putting anything into the barrel.

A 169   How did they do it?

Riddle 4

B 176   A man lived on the twelfth floor of an apartment building.

C 183   Each day, when he came home from work, he took the elevator to the eighth floor, got out, and walked up to his apartment on the twelfth floor.

A 190   The elevator was in good operating order and went all the way to the twelfth floor.

D 197   Why did the man walk up those four flights of stairs?

Structured Experience 150

151. CASH REGISTER:
GROUP DECISION MAKING

Goals

    I. To demonstrate how decision making is improved by consensus seeking.

    II. To explore the impact that assumptions have on decision making.

Group Size

An unlimited number of groups of five to seven participants each.

Time Required

Approximately thirty minutes.

Materials

    I. A copy of the Cash Register Worksheet for each participant and for each group.

    II. A pencil for each participant.

Physical Setting

A room large enough for groups and individuals to work without being distracted or overheard by others.

Process

    I. The facilitator gives one copy of the Cash Register Worksheet to each participant. He instructs participants that they have five minutes to read "The Story" paragraph and then to indicate whether each of the "Statements About the Story" is *true, false,* or *unknown* (indicated by a question mark).

    II. The facilitator forms groups of five to seven members each. He gives each group one copy of the Cash Register Worksheet and indicates that each group has approximately ten minutes to reach consensus on whether each statement is true, false, or unknown.

    III. The facilitator announces the "correct" answers. (Statement 3 is false, statement 6 is true, and all other statements are unknown.)

    IV. The facilitator leads a brief discussion of the experience, during which he elicits comments from participants about making assumptions and about the values of group decision making.

   V. Each participant writes at least two implications of the experience for "back-home" application. These statements are shared with the group.

Variations

   I. Step I can be omitted.

   II. Another "ambiguous" story can be used.

   III. The process of consensus seeking can be discussed from the perspectives of "giving up" points of view and of feelings experienced.

Similar Structured Experiences: *Vol. I:* Structured Experiences **11, 15;** *Vol. II:* **30;** *Vol. III:* **64;** *'72 Annual:* **84;** *Vol. IV:* **115;** *'75 Annual:* **140;** *Vol. V:* **155, 157.**
Lecturette Source: *'73 Annual:* "Synergy and Consensus-Seeking."

Notes on the Use of "Cash Register":

Based on materials in William V. Haney, *Communication and Organizational Behavior* (3rd ed.), Homewood, Ill.: Richard D. Irwin, 1973. Used with permission of the author.

Structured Experience 151

CASH REGISTER WORKSHEET

The Story

A businessman had just turned off the lights in the store when a man appeared and demanded money. The owner opened a cash register. The contents of the cash register were scooped up, and the man sped away. A member of the police force was notified promptly.

Statements About the Story

1. A man appeared after the owner had turned off his store lights.   T   F   ?

2. The robber was a *man*.   T   F   ?

3. The man did not demand money.   T   F   ?

4. The man who opened the cash register was the owner.   T   F   ?

5. The store owner scooped up the contents of the cash register and ran away.   T   F   ?

6. Someone opened a cash register.   T   F   ?

7. After the man who demanded the money scooped up the contents of the cash register, he ran away.   T   F   ?

8. While the cash register contained money, the story does *not* state *how much*.   T   F   ?

9. The robber demanded money of the owner.   T   F   ?

10. The story concerns a series of events in which only three persons are referred to: the owner of the store, a man who demanded money, and a member of the police force.   T   F   ?

11. The following events in the story are true: someone demanded money, a cash register was opened, its contents were scooped up, and a man dashed out of the store.   T   F   ?

152. HELPING RELATIONSHIPS: VERBAL AND NONVERBAL COMMUNICATION

Goals

I. To demonstrate the effects of posturing and eye contact on helping relationships.

II. To focus group members' attention on the impact of their nonverbal behaviors on other individuals.

III. To teach basic nonverbal listening and attending skills.

Group Size

No more than twenty participants.

Time Required

Approximately thirty minutes.

Physical Setting

Movable chairs and open space.

Process

I. The facilitator introduces the experience by discussing the verbal and nonverbal aspects of communication, pointing out that although individuals seem to rely primarily on verbal cues in their interactions, nonverbal cues (gestures, posture, tone of voice, etc.) are also important in communication. To reinforce this point, he demonstrates how nonverbal cues can either contradict or confirm a verbal message. To demonstrate *contradiction*, he approaches a group member and says, "I like you," with his voice raised in anger and his hands clenched into fists. To demonstrate *confirmation*, he approaches the group member and says, "I like you," in a warm manner, followed by a hug.

II. The facilitator announces that the activity will consist of forming dyads and exploring the effects of different seating arrangements. He explains that the members of each dyad will sit in different positions and that as they assume each position, they are to remain silent and be aware of the effect of that seating arrangement.

III. Participants form dyads, and the facilitator directs them to sit back to back without talking. After the dyads have been sitting in this position for about a minute, the facilitator directs them to sit side by side. After another minute, he directs them to sit face to face.

IV. After another minute, each dyad discusses its reactions to the activity. The facilitator elicits observations about the experience from the entire group.

V. The dyads are seated face to face and silently assume three body postures (one minute each): slouched, straight, and leaning forward.

VI. Each dyad then discusses its reactions to the preceding round. The facilitator elicits observations about the experience from the entire group.

VII. One partner assumes the role of helpee; the other partner assumes the role of helper.

VIII. While seated face to face, the dyads silently experience three different eye-contact situations (one minute each):
   1. The helper attempts to look the helpee in the eye while the helpee looks down or away.
   2. The helpee attempts to look the helper in the eye while the helper looks down or away.
   3. The helper and the helpee have direct eye-to-eye contact.

IX. Step VI is repeated.

X. After processing the eye-contact experience, the facilitator leads a discussion of the participants' overall reactions to the sequence of activities. He focuses the discussion on the integration and application of this learning.

Variations

I. Participants can be permitted to talk at any time during the experience. The talking may include counseling on "real" problems.

II. In the face-to-face situation, participants can be directed to move their chairs to a distance that is most comfortable for them.

III. The process can be combined with a "fishbowl" design. One dyad is seated in the center of the group and goes through the activity sequence. The other group members are instructed to observe the impact of the different positionings and to report their observations.

IV. Different dyads can be formed for each round of the activity.

Similar Structured Experiences: *Vol. I:* Structured Experience 22; *Vol. II:* **44**; *Vol. III:* **50, 65, 72.**

Suggested Instrument: *'73 Annual:* "Helping Relationship Inventory."

Lecturette Sources: *'72 Annual:* "Communication Modes: An Experiential Lecture"; *'74 Annual:* "'Don't You Think That . . . ?': An Experiential Lecture on Indirect and Direct Communication"; *'75 Annual:* "Nonverbal Communication and the Intercultural Encounter."

References

Danish, S. J., & Hauer, A. L. *Helping skills: A basic training program.* New York: Behavioral Publications, 1973.

Ivey, A. E. *Microcounseling: Innovations in interviewing training.* Springfield, Ill.: Charles C Thomas, 1971.

Notes on the Use of "Helping Relationships":

Submitted by Clarke G. Carney.

Structured Experience 152

153. BABEL: INTERPERSONAL COMMUNICATION

Goals

I. To examine language barriers, which contribute to breakdowns in communication.

II. To demonstrate the anxieties and frustrations that may be felt when communicating under difficult circumstances.

III. To illustrate the impact of nonverbal communication when verbal communication is ineffective and/or restricted.

Group Size

An unlimited number of equal-sized groups of four, six, or eight members each.

Time Required

Approximately two hours.

Physical Setting

A room large enough for the groups to meet comfortably.

Materials

I. A pencil and paper for each participant.

II. A blindfold for each group member.

Process

I. The facilitator divides the large group into subgroups.

II. When the groups have assembled, the facilitator announces that each group is to create a language of its own. This language must be significantly different from English and must include the following:
   1. a greeting
   2. a description of some object, person, or event
   3. an evaluative statement about an object or a person
   4. a farewell.
Group members must be able to "speak" their group's language at the end of this step. (Forty-five minutes.)

III. Within each language group, members number themselves sequentially, i.e., 1, 2, 3, 4, etc. The facilitator announces the location of a new group to be composed of all participants numbered 1. He likewise forms new groups of participants numbered 2, 3, 4, and so on.

IV. The facilitator directs members to pair off in the new groups. Each member must teach his new language to his partner without using English or any other recognized language. (Twenty minutes.)

V. The facilitator distributes a blindfold to each group. A blindfolded volunteer from each group teaches his language to the group. A second volunteer repeats this task. (Twenty minutes.)

VI. The facilitator distributes blindfolds to all remaining participants. Participants are told to stand in their second groups, and all chairs are moved aside. Participants blindfold themselves and are instructed to find their original groups without the use of any conventional language or people's names.

VII. When the original groups have been re-formed, the facilitator instructs them to discuss the activity and to answer the following questions:
   1. What did this experience illustrate about communication?
   2. How did you feel during the experience?
   3. What did you learn about yourself from it?

VIII. The facilitator leads a general discussion on the problems faced by people who do not understand a language and on the difficulties that blind people may have in communicating.

Variations

I. The requirements for the new vocabulary can be changed to make the task more difficult or less difficult.

II. All participants can be blindfolded for step V.

III. Real languages can be used. The phrases can be preset.

Similar Structured Experience: *'74 Annual:* Structured Experience **125.**
Suggested Instrument: *'74 Annual:* "Interpersonal Communication Inventory."
Lecturette Source: *'75 Annual:* "Nonverbal Communication and the Intercultural Encounter."

Submitted by Philip M. Ericson.

Structured Experience 153

Notes on the Use of "Babel":

154. STYLES OF LEADERSHIP: A SERIES OF ROLE PLAYS

Goals

I. To explore the impact that leaders have on decision making in groups.

II. To demonstrate the effects of hidden agendas.

Group Size

Two groups of five persons each. (Multiple pairs of groups can be directed simultaneously in the same room.)

Time Required

Approximately two hours.

Materials

I. A copy of the Styles of Leadership Information Sheet for each participant.

II. For each member of group A, a different Styles of Leadership Role Sheet for Act I.

III. For each member of group B, a different Styles of Leadership Role Sheet for Act II.

IV. A copy of the Styles of Leadership Debriefing Sheet for Act I and a copy of the Styles of Leadership Debriefing Sheet for Act II for each participant.

V. A name tag ("Leader," "Member One," "Member Two," "Member Three," and "Member Four") for each role player in each of the two groups.

Physical Setting

A room large enough to accommodate role playing and discussion.

Process

I. Each participant receives a copy of the Styles of Leadership Information Sheet.

II. The facilitator designates two groups, A and B, and announces that group A will role play Act I (scenes 1 through 6) while group B observes. He hands each member of group A a name tag and the appropriate Styles of Leadership Role Sheet for Act I and allows five minutes for the participants to study their roles for scene 1.

He hands each member of group B a copy of the Styles of Leadership Debriefing Sheet for Act I. The facilitator ascertains that members understand their role instructions.

III. The five members of group A role play the six scenes of Act I. Members of group B observe the role-play interaction. (After each five-minute scene, the facilitator instructs participants to study briefly their roles for the next scene.) The facilitator solicits brief comments from the observers after scenes 2, 4, and 6.

IV. The facilitator distributes a copy of the Styles of Leadership Debriefing Sheet for Act I to each member of group A and conducts a debriefing session. The facilitator and the members of both groups discuss the type of behavior portrayed by the leader in scene 1 and the impact he had on decision making in the group. All participants then discuss similar tendencies or actions that they have observed in other groups. The discussion then focuses on leader characteristics displayed in each of the other scenes in turn. The facilitator makes sure that the discussion focuses on the attitudes portrayed and not on how well the role players portrayed them.

V. Steps II through IV are repeated, this time with members of group B role playing Act II while members of group A observe.

Variations

I. Some scenes can be omitted.

II. The content can be adapted to a particular client group.

III. Members of the observing group can be assigned specific tasks such as observing a particular individual or a particular set of behaviors.

Similar Structured Experiences: *Vol. I:* Structured Experiences **3, 9**; *'75 Annual:* **138**; *Vol. V:* **159, 162.**

Suggested Instruments: *'72 Annual:* "Supervisory Attitudes: The X-Y Scale"; *'73 Annual:* "LEAD (Leadership: Employee-Orientation and Differentiation) Questionnaire"; *'75 Annual:* "Decision-Style Inventory."

Lecturette Sources: *'74 Annual:* "Hidden Agendas," "The 'Shouldist' Manager," "Individual Needs and Organizational Goals: An Experiential Lecture."

Submitted by Gerald M. Phillips.

Notes on the Use of "Styles of Leadership":

Structured Experience 154

STYLES OF LEADERSHIP INFORMATION SHEET

Background

The setting for the role play is Cartersburg, a Northeastern city with a population of about 200,000. Like most cities of its kind, Cartersburg has been the scene of increasing trouble with gangs of young people: vandalism, street fighting, and considerable harassment of citizens and police.

Contact has been made with most of the major street gangs, and they have agreed to participate in a program to make Cartersburg a safer city. But the situation is still insecure, and the gangs are perfectly willing to slip back into their old patterns if the city administration does not "put up."

To date, the results have not been significant. Not much has been done, although there has been a lot of talk. There are only a few social workers offering personal and vocational counseling in the neighborhoods. There is no central coordinating office, and the amount of money available to support the program is tenuous. The city administration hopes for a Federal grant while the young people expect the city to pay for the program out of ongoing revenues. The editor of the city's only newspaper supports local financing, but many prominent citizens have declared that the problem is a national one. Some efforts have been made to get financial contributions, but since there is no general coordinating agency, no one knows to whom to contribute.

The mayor, aware of growing dissatisfaction and the possibility of renewed violence, has appointed five prominent citizens to a Committee for Community Action. Their charge is to study the problems of young people and then to present a list of programs that might provide solutions. They have not been asked to figure out a budget, merely to identify possible solutions. The committee has met several times, and at this point it should be ready to draft recommendations to be presented to the mayor.

Instructions

Read your role sheet carefully and, insofar as possible, try to *be* the person described on that sheet. It is particularly important that you represent the *point of view* on the card.

STYLES OF LEADERSHIP ROLE SHEET FOR ACT I

Leader

Scene 1. You favor increased police protection in the neighborhoods. You know this is the ONLY solution. Resist all efforts by members of your group to suggest anything else. See how quickly you can get them to discuss a specific plan for police enforcement. DO NOT LET THEM SERIOUSLY CONSIDER ANY OTHER PROPOSAL.

Scene 2. The only way to operate a group is to let all factions be heard. It really isn't the leader's place to intervene and direct the discussion. They may be having some problems, but this is something they will have to work out for themselves. And why is Member Four picking on you? You might appeal to the other members to get him off your back.

Scene 3. Member One is a real nuisance. There is no point in trying to accomplish anything in this group until we are rid of him. Do anything, promise anything, but get the rest of the group to support you in ousting Member One from the committee.

Scene 4. Parliamentary procedure is the order of the day. Make these guys follow the parliamentary line. Every time someone states an idea, see if you can get it in the form of a motion so that it can be formally debated and disposed of. You have had a lot of experience as a chairman, and this newfangled "group dynamics" annoys you.

Scene 5. Members One and Two look uneasy. You can't have a group until you have group harmony. We have got to know each other better before we get on with business. We have got to be friends, to feel comfortable with one another. Let's just use this meeting to find out more about each other. We don't dare do any business until we really get to know each other.

Scene 6. You can't tackle a problem until all the facts are in. There simply hasn't been enough research on the problem. The local university has a staff available that could do a competent job of studying the problem. A research plan and some grant money to support investigations are what we need. When a systematic investigation has been completed, then we can talk about solutions. This meeting should develop the research plan.

Structured Experience 154

STYLES OF LEADERSHIP ROLE SHEET FOR ACT I

Member One

Scene 1. One possible alternative is to develop some kind of honor policing in the neighborhoods. You are not really sure what form this should take, but you are sure that bringing in regular police would seriously inflame an already dangerous situation. Try to get some of the other members to comment on your proposal.

Scene 2. Member Two is strictly an administration man. He opposes your idea for bringing in Vista volunteers. He is probably the mayor's brother-in-law. Even if he seems to be supporting you, don't let him get away with it because he is really against you.

Scene 3. Member Two has been on your block for a long time. You have been fighting him for many years and you know what kind of dirty fighter he is. You may have to have a head-on confrontation with him before the group can get on with its work.

Scene 4. You are interested in a vocational training program, but you don't want to leap into it until you have had a chance to talk it over thoroughly with others in the group. Resist jumping to a conclusion. Don't let the leader railroad your idea. The dynamics of the group demand consensus. This is not a question that can be handled by parliamentary procedure.

Scene 5. The situation is critical. We have got to get something going or we will have gang fights and vandalism again. If this meeting doesn't decide something, we have had it. Let's get some results—almost any results. Particularly, we had better make some recommendations about police.

Scene 6. The problem has been studied to death and no one seems to want to do anything. Probably someone will suggest even more research. You are impatient. You want at least three substantive proposals to come out of this meeting: (1) a street recreation program, (2) aid to neighborhood merchants, and (3) a family counseling and crisis-intervention service. You are perfectly willing to support any other ideas. Remember, all this committee has to do is refer the ideas.

STYLES OF LEADERSHIP ROLE SHEET FOR ACT I

Member Two

Scene 1. Job training is what is needed. You cannot solve a problem without working on the cause. These kids are unemployed; if they were working, they wouldn't be on the streets. You think the committee should investigate the job market and propose on-the-job training programs. You realize, however, that some stopgap programs may be necessary.

Scene 2. Member One is a radical. Sometimes, but not often, he has good ideas. You are suspicious of his suggestion to bring in Vista volunteers because it could result in radical Federal intervention. Furthermore, you think a community recreation program is a better idea. Push your program, but if the going gets rough, Member One may be a possible ally (if you can get him to do some log rolling with you).

Scene 3. Member One is a dangerous radical. He can disrupt any group he is in. See who you can get to support you in throwing him out of the group because, until he is out, nothing will get done.

Scene 4. You are interested in the vocational training proposals Member One is making, but you have some doubts about the practical aspects of the program. It would be a good idea if this committee pooled its knowledge about vocational training before deciding that it will be the program proposed. See if you can get specific ideas from Member One about what he is proposing. Talk to him directly, but do not debate the issue with him. Avoid a majority/minority split. This committee must have *consensus*.

Scene 5. Police protection is not the answer. It is necessary to develop community spirit and concern for the welfare of the whole city. People like Member One who advocate police protection are probably racist, but you agree with him that something needs to be done. Debate the police protection issue and do not let anyone sidetrack you.

Scene 6. This is a tough problem and you wish you had never accepted service on this committee. All the proposed programs confuse you. It might really be a good thing to have more research done.

Structured Experience 154

STYLES OF LEADERSHIP ROLE SHEET FOR ACT I

Member Three

Scene 1. Money! How can we get money to operate the program? Whatever solution is offered, make sure you cross-examine the proposer until you find out where the money is coming from.

Scene 2. How did these other guys get on this committee anyway? Member One is an idealistic fool and all Member Two wants is some jobs for his relatives. You don't know Member Four from Adam, and none of them are very interested in your proposal for a street literacy-training program and a program in black studies. Make sure you are heard. You are the *only* one in the group who has any firsthand knowledge of the problem anyway.

Scene 3. Members One and Two seem to be fighting and the leader seems to be taking sides. See what you can do to get these guys calmed down so that the group can get on with its work.

Scene 4. You are somewhat suspicious of vocational training programs because you have no evidence that they work. You are perfectly willing to talk about them for a while to see if such evidence exists. Ask all the questions you need to. Don't let the other members panic and push you into premature decisions. Work this out slowly.

Scene 5. Discussing police protection is a waste of time. Any damn fool knows we need protection. But we need preventive measures. This group ought to brainstorm the problems that people in the rough neighborhoods are having and come up with an overwhelming list of ideas. Let's do the brainstorming so we can get at the issues.

Scene 6. Get immediate acceptance for the following: (1) a program for improved police protection, including neighborhood volunteers; (2) a program for vocational training outside of the schools; (3) an expanded neighborhood recreation program; (4) establishment of neighborhood protection councils, including an underwriting feature; (5) support for local merchants whose properties have been damaged; and (6) legislation to curb rioting and gang warfare. Get the group to accept this manifesto.

STYLES OF LEADERSHIP ROLE SHEET FOR ACT I

Member Four

Scene 1. Hey, how about this leader? He is pretty damned authoritarian, isn't he? Why won't he let other people talk about what they need to talk about? Maybe he needs a good critique of his leadership, administered by you.

Scene 2. So Member Three is a black activist! These guys are trying to ruin the neighborhood. Thrift and concern for the home are what are needed. Actually, all this fuss about the underprivileged is foolish. If they want to live in filth and beat each other up, you see no reason why they shouldn't be permitted to do it. If you can get the leader to agree with you, maybe you can end this meeting without proposing some silly and expensive program that no one wants. Push the leader; talk him into agreeing with you even if you have to interrupt while others are talking.

Scene 3. Members One and Two seem to be fighting and the leader seems to be taking sides. See what you can do to get these guys calmed down so that the group can get on with its work.

Scene 4. You have had considerable experience with vocational training programs and you know of many difficulties that have to be solved before such programs will work. First, vocational needs have to be surveyed. The schools have to support the idea. You need support from industry, etc. Raise these issues one at a time and do not let anyone push you into a decision until you have had a chance to consider these and other issues at length.

Scene 5. Why is everyone in such a hurry to get down to business? We had better get to know each other before we try to work out the problems. After all, if we don't trust each other, we won't get far. The leader seems to be suggesting this. Help him get it going. Otherwise, these dogmatists will push through their ideas. Incidentally, maybe a little sensitivity training will help things in the neighborhoods, too.

Scene 6. Is it really possible to get *all* the facts about anything? Some of the people in the group are too impatient. On the other hand, if too much time is taken, nothing will get done. See if you can reconcile the two factions.

Structured Experience 154

STYLES OF LEADERSHIP DEBRIEFING SHEET FOR ACT I

Scene 1 features the "know-it-all" chairman. He has all the ideas; the members' suggestions are worthless. The group is used by him only to ratify his ideas, and any ideas proposed by the group are regarded as rebellion.

Scene 2 shows the laissez-faire leader carried to an extreme. He exerts no leadership at all, not even as a traffic director.

Scene 3 shows the leader attempting to manipulate the members into helping him handle some of his own personal problems with the group.

Scene 4 puts an efficiency expert in charge of the group. He holds to parliamentary procedure, and the procedure is more important than the ideas.

Scene 5 shows the social director/sensitivity trainer in charge. He is much more interested in personal developments in the group than he is in the agenda.

Scene 6 shows the influence of research on problem solving. The reverence for research supersedes the need for a solution. The myth of the grant subverts the group.

STYLES OF LEADERSHIP ROLE SHEET FOR ACT II

Leader

Scene 7. Being a committee chairman is a means to power. What you need is a bigger constituency. Member One has a good idea. The appointment of a general supervisory committee with you at the head would give you more power. You could fill that committee with your friends and thus have two organizations to support you when you run for re-election next year. Make sure this committee gets proposed.

Scene 8. Things are moving much too rapidly. This group just seems to want to jump to a conclusion. Things are not really as bad as people say they are. There haven't been any riots in your suburb. Slow this group down. Don't just let them grab at any idea and push it through. Suggest investigation, consideration of all possibilities, letting all sides be heard, fairness, democracy, and the American way. Everything must be considered. Don't let them get anything by you.

Scene 9. Why can't this group get on the road? Member One has some good ideas. Push him to propose their adoption. Try to get them through. What kind of business is this—a high-powered group like this, and no action? If you don't get something done at this meeting, they will be very angry downtown; the press will be on your back and you won't be the mayor's good buddy any more. Make sure you get the group to adopt a proposal, even if you have to invent it.

Scene 10. Why is everyone against me? Everyone wants to lead the group. Well, dammit, I am the leader and we are not moving one more step until I am sure this is fully recognized. I will not let anyone push me out of this chair.

Scene 11. Before we go on, we need an agenda. We need to set priorities and we need to get them in order for formal consideration. Do not let the meeting go on until the group decides on an order for consideration of all the ideas that have been presented.

Scene 12. We have spent too much time on this committee. It is dangerous to make proposals since it is likely that the committee that makes them will have to carry them out. Get the experts at city hall to take over and get this committee disbanded at this meeting.

STYLES OF LEADERSHIP ROLE SHEET FOR ACT II

Member One

Scene 7. You propose a general supervisory committee to be appointed by the mayor *before* substantive proposals are made. You have decided that it is pointless just to study proposals. The proposals need to be worked out, and a general supervisory committee would accomplish this. Such a prominent public committee would also put the brakes on radical proposals. Spell out the details and demand that nothing more be done until the mayor appoints the committee.

Scene 8. After careful consideration, you have decided that neighborhood papers are necessary to keep people posted on local events and to dispel rumors. The papers can be put into business with an expenditure of $16,000 and can be supported by local advertising. There is an editor with experience available. You know the mayor favors this proposal. Get going.

Scene 9. You have a lot of ideas on this matter: policing, minority groups on the police force, neighborhood newspapers, job training, recreation, school improvement, etc., but you need time to sift them through. Don't be premature. The only thing worse than no proposal would be the wrong proposal at the wrong time, so don't let anyone push you into a decision.

Scene 10. The leader is a hopeless neurotic. You would make a better leader. See if you can get the group to support you.

Scene 11. The most important thing is police protection. Make sure that it gets top priority.

Scene 12. This committee is a great idea. It takes the whole business out of the hands of city hall. It would be best if this committee had the power to implement its ideas. You can't trust city hall.

STYLES OF LEADERSHIP ROLE SHEET FOR ACT II

Member Two

Scene 7. You have three proposals to make: (1) improvement of police by recruitment of neighborhood people for the force, (2) on-the-job training to be offered by local industry for minority groups, and (3) establishment of a neighborhood newspaper to keep rumors under control. Push these ideas. Resist any slowdown.

Scene 8. Member One has a great idea. Support him. Go beyond him. Call for more money. Call for improved policing. Call for a recreation program. Call for improvement of the schools. And make absolutely sure that Member One gets his newspaper idea through.

Scene 9. Go slow. You are entirely open and neutral, but any idea that does come up ought to be looked at carefully for a week before adoption. Resist any attempts to get anything concrete passed at this meeting.

Scene 10. Member One seems to want to take over as leader. He would make a better leader than the one you have now. Support him and try to get him voted in as leader.

Scene 11. The most important thing to talk about is job training. Make sure the group deals with that first. Police protection is a dangerous idea. Make sure they don't talk about that at all.

Scene 12. It really is irrelevant who is responsible for the program just so long as there is a program. Pass all these ideas: improved police protection, recreation facilities, summer programs for youth. Get at least one idea adopted tonight.

Structured Experience 154

STYLES OF LEADERSHIP ROLE SHEET FOR ACT II

Member Three

Scene 7. Member Two has great ideas. Give him all the support you can.

Scene 8. You have heard that there is $20,000 immediately available for any good idea. If you hear about one with that kind of price tag, support it.

Scene 9. Go slow. You are entirely open and neutral, but any idea that does come up ought to be looked at carefully for a week before adoption. Resist any attempts to get anything concrete passed at this meeting.

Scene 10. You are really interested in getting a proposal adopted at this meeting and everyone else keeps playing "king of the hill." Push for a proposal related to police protection and do everything you can to get it adopted.

Scene 11. The most important thing to talk about is protection of property. You want to form an association of merchants in each of the neighborhoods. Police protection ideas are dangerous and job training is too slow. Be sure the merchants' association gets top billing.

Scene 12. The leader is trying to pass the buck. Get him involved with some of the programs proposed by Member Two.

STYLES OF LEADERSHIP ROLE SHEET FOR ACT II

Member Four

Scene 7. What is the leader trying to do? You know he is a master politician. Is he trying to build a new political base for himself? When he supports the supervisory committee idea, accuse him of using it for his own personal gains and see what happens.

Scene 8. You have heard that there is $20,000 available immediately for any good idea. If you hear of one with that kind of price tag, support it intensely.

Scene 9. Why is the leader trying to railroad the group? Could it be that he is worried about what the newspapers will say about him? Raise this idea and see what happens.

Scene 10. It looks like Member One is trying to take over the group. The leader you have is perfectly O. K. with you. Give him your support and put Member One in his place (which is outside the meeting).

Scene 11. How long are these jokers going to talk about what we should talk about? All the ideas are O. K. Let's pass them and get this damn meeting over with. It is a waste of time to talk about priorities and agendas.

Scene 12. What a bore. Can't we get this meeting over with so we can all go home and watch the game on television?

STYLES OF LEADERSHIP DEBRIEFING SHEET FOR ACT II

Scene 7 features a rampant power play. The leader has political designs and his prime concern is getting the group to help him play them out.

Scene 8 shows the effects of excessive caution. The leader here is afraid of action because he is afraid of the responsibility it will put on him.

Scene 9 is an old-fashioned railroad. The leader has some urgency, which lies outside the group purview, about getting something done, and he will do it whether the group wants it or not.

Scene 10 puts a neurotic, mildly paranoid person in the chair. It shows how power plays within the group can subvert action.

Scene 11 shows how adherence to the formalities of group operation can get in the way of decision making and how agenda can sometimes interfere with progress.

Scene 12 is an example of passing the buck by a leader who does not want to take responsibility.

Structured Experience 154

155. SALES PUZZLE: INFORMATION SHARING

Goals

   I. To explore the effects of collaboration and competition in group problem solving.

   II. To study how information is shared by members of a work group.

   III. To observe problem-solving strategies within a group.

Group Size

An unlimited number of groups of five participants each.

Time Required

Approximately one hour.

Materials

   I. A Sales Puzzle Problem Sheet for each participant.

   II. Three different Sales Puzzle Clue Strips for each member of a group, so that each group receives all fifteen clues.

   III. Pencils and paper or newsprint and felt-tipped markers for each group.

Physical Setting

A room large enough to allow the groups to work without distracting one another.

Process

   I. The facilitator introduces the experience as a problem-solving task, but he does not discuss techniques or procedures that may be used.

   II. Groups of five persons each are formed; additional persons serve as observers.

   III. Each participant receives a copy of the Sales Puzzle Problem Sheet. The facilitator reads it aloud and ascertains that all members understand the task. He gives a set of the fifteen Sales Puzzle Clue Strips to each group, three to each member. He informs the groups that they will have thirty minutes to solve the problem.

   IV. If one group finishes before time is called, the facilitator may instruct those members to observe other groups still in process. Observers do not communicate in any way with members of working groups.

V. When all groups have reached a solution, or at the end of thirty minutes, the facilitator leads a discussion of the process. Special emphasis is given to such points as the following:
1. the effects of collaboration and competition
2. the sharing of information among group members
3. the techniques or strategies employed in problem solving
4. the emergence of leadership and the level of contribution of group members.

VI. The facilitator announces the answer to the puzzle. (He may post the key for all to see.) A general discussion of the experience follows.

Variations

I. Groups of six can be formed, with one member of each group designated as an observer. The observers can be permitted to make process interventions at any time.

II. The material can be adapted to fit a particular client group.

III. The design can be used as an intergroup-competition activity.

IV. Roles can be assigned to particular individuals within groups.

Sales Puzzle Key

Ranking	Northeast Mr. Black	Southeast Mr. White	Northwest Mr. Blue	Southwest Mr. Grey
First	commercial	distribution	GOVERNMENT	INDUSTRIAL
Second	INDUSTRIAL	GOVERNMENT	distribution	commercial
Third	DISTRIBUTION	industrial	COMMERCIAL	government
Fourth	government	COMMERCIAL	industrial	DISTRIBUTION

Capital letters: information given to the groups.
Lower-case letters: information to be deduced by the groups.

The matrix does not have to take this particular form for the correct answer to be reached. However, some plan of organizing the information—such as a matrix—will speed the solution.

Statements on the Sales Puzzle Problem Sheet not relevant to solution: numbers 1, 6, 9, 11, 13.

Structured Experience 155

Similar Structured Experiences: *'72 Annual:* Structured Experience **80;** *Vol. IV:* **117;** *Vol. V:* **156.**

Lecturette Source: *'73 Annual:* "Win/Lose Situations."

Notes on the Use of "Sales Puzzle":

SALES PUZZLE PROBLEM SHEET

Background

A certain company has four regional sales districts: Northeast, Northwest, Southeast, and Southwest.

The district sales managers meet quarterly to report on their sales in four categories: commercial, distribution, industrial, and government.

The managers' names are: Mr. Grey, Mr. Blue, Mr. Black, and Mr. White.

At their most recent meeting, the managers discovered that each had his highest sales in a different category from the others. In other words, one of them ranked highest in commercial sales, another had the highest distribution sales, a third had the most industrial sales, and the last topped the list in government sales.

Instructions

Your group's task is to determine the regional sales district in which each manager works and to determine the category in which he had the highest sales, the second highest sales, and so on.

Each member of your group has received three clues to the puzzle. There is a total of fifteen clues.

You may share verbally all the information you have, but *do not allow other members to read your clues.*

SALES PUZZLE CLUE STRIPS

1. Mr. Black was the host for this meeting.

----

2. The Southeast manager was urged to "get out of the cellar" in commercial sales.

----

3. Mr. White was congratulated for climbing to first place in distribution sales.

----

4. Mr. Blue said that he would host the next meeting in Portland, Oregon.

----

5. The Southwest manager came in first in industrial sales for the first time.

----

6. Mr. Grey was the only manager who brought his wife.

----

7. Everyone kidded the Southwest manager, who came in last in distribution sales.

----

8. The Northwest manager was, as usual, third in commercial sales.

----

9. The Southwest manager had to leave the meeting early.

----

10. The Southwest manager had to pay off a five-dollar bet to the Northeast manager because the Northeast was one place ahead in distribution sales. (But he won it back at golf.)

----

11. Mr. White had a bad cold, so he didn't play golf.

----

12. The Northwest manager explained his coming in first in government sales (over the Southeast) by a big order from the Denver Federal Service Center.

----

13. Mr. Blue was the big winner at poker.

----

14. Everyone was surprised that the Northeast manager slipped to second place in industrial sales, since most industry is in that area.

----

15. Mr. Grey won the pot for the golf game.

----

156. ROOM 703: INFORMATION SHARING

Goals

I. To explore the effects of collaboration and competition in group problem solving.

II. To study how task-relevant information is shared within a work group.

III. To observe group strategies for problem solving.

Group Size

An unlimited number of groups of six.

Time Required

Thirty to forty-five minutes.

Materials

I. A set of six Room 703 Basic Information Cards for each group. Each card is coded by the number of dots (from one to six) following the first sentence on the card. Each of the six cards contains different data from the other cards.

II. Paper and a pencil for each participant.

III. Masking tape.

Physical Setting

A room large enough for the groups to work without influencing each other.

Process

I. The facilitator distributes a set of Room 703 Basic Information Cards to each group, one card to each member. Three minutes is allowed for members to study the information.

II. Groups are instructed to begin working. (Twenty minutes.)

III. When there is agreement within a group that the solution has been reached, the group discusses how it organized to accomplish its task.

IV. The facilitator elicits comments from each of the groups on its problem-solving process.

V. The facilitator calls for each group's solution and then announces the correct solution:

Periods

		1	2	3	4
	700	Mr. Jones	Mr. Lee	Ms. Martin	Mr. Jacobs
	701	Mr. Jacobs	Ms. Martin	Mr. Lee	Mr. Jones
Rooms	702	Ms. Martin	Mr. Jones	Mr. Jacobs	Mr. Lee
	703	**Mr. Lee**	**Mr. Jacobs**	**Mr. Jones**	**Ms. Martin**

He may post the answer chart and inform the members that the solution can be reached by:

1. Making a blank chart similar to the one displayed.
2. Filling in the names of the teachers who are known to be in certain rooms during certain class periods from information provided on the Room 703 Basic Information Cards. (This process is aided by using the clues to make one list of teachers and another list of aides, in order to differentiate between the two.)
3. Using deductive reasoning to fill in the names of other teachers in each of the spaces, so that each teacher is in a different room during each of the four periods.

VI. The facilitator presents a lecturette on the concept of shared information and leadership.

Variations

I. The problem can be made more difficult by adding more irrelevant information.

II. The Room 703 Basic Information Cards can be rewritten to contain material more specific to the particular participant group. The formula is simple: begin at the end, with a correct solution, and apportion data to participants so that each has a critical piece of information as well as common knowledge.

III. Additional participants can be accommodated within the groups by duplicating information cards. For example, if there are eight members, two participants receive the card with one period at the end of the first sentence, and two receive the card with two periods.

IV. The problem-solving phase can be interrupted several times for processing. Participants can be instructed to rate their confidence in the correctness of the solution and their satisfaction with the work style of the group.

V. The facilitator may give any of the following hints:
  1. "Discover who the educational aides are."
  2. "Discover who the teachers are."
  3. "Deductive reasoning should be applied to the problem."

Similar Structured Experiences: *Vol. II:* Structured Experiences **29, 31**; *'72 Annual:* **80**; *Vol. IV:* **102, 103, 117**; *Vol. V:* **155**.

Suggested Instrument: *'74 Annual:* "S-C (Student-Content) Teaching Inventory."

Lecturette Sources: *'73 Annual:* "Win/Lose Situations," "Synergy and Consensus-Seeking."

Notes on the Use of "Room 703":

Submitted by John R. Joachim.

Structured Experience 156

ROOM 703 BASIC INFORMATION CARDS

You may tell your group what is on this card, but do not pass it around for others to read.

Information:

Room 701 has Mr. Lee for a teacher during the third period.

Mr. Jones and Ms. Carr do not get along well, so they do not work together.

During the first period, the team leader, whom Harry likes, teaches Room 702.

You may tell your group what is on this card, but do not pass it around for others to read . .

Information:

All teachers teach at the same time and exchange groups at the end of each period.

Each teacher likes a different group best. During the second period, each teacher teaches the group he or she likes best.

Each teacher teaches each group during one of the first four periods of the day.

You may tell your group what is on this card, but do not pass it around for others to read. . .

Information:

The Robert E. Lucas Intermediate School has two teachers' aides, four teachers, and four groups of students.

Ms. Martin is the team leader for the Intermediate Unit.

Mr. Lee likes to work with room 700.

Mr. Jones teaches room 701 during the fourth period but he likes room 702 best.

You may tell your group what is on this card, but do not pass it around for others to read. . . .

Information:

Your group members have all the information needed to find the answer to the following question:

> In what sequence are the teachers (by name) in room 703 during the first four periods?

Only one answer is correct and you can prove it.

Some of the information your group has is irrelevant and will not help to solve this problem.

You may tell your group what is on this card, but do not pass it around for others to read. . . . .

Information:

Ms. Carr and Mr. Jacobs disagree about how it would be best to handle room 702, in which there seems to be a history of abusing substitute teachers.

The team leader has been at the Robert E. Lucas Intermediate School for five years.

You may tell your group what is on this card, but do not pass it around for others to read. . . . . .

Information:

The team leader teaches room 701 during the second period.

Harry works with room 702 during the second period.

Ms. Martin has been at the Robert E. Lucas School for the shortest period of time.

---

157. LETTER OCCURRENCE/HEALTH PROFESSIONS PRESTIGE: CONSENSUS-SEEKING TASKS

Goals

I. To compare decisions made by individuals with those made by groups.

II. To teach effective consensus-seeking techniques.

III. To demonstrate the phenomenon of synergy.

Group Size

Groups of five to twelve members each. Several groups may be directed simultaneously in the same room. (Synergy is more likely to be achieved with smaller groups, i.e., five to seven members.)

Time Required

Approximately one hour per task.

Materials

I. A pencil for each participant.

II. A copy of the Letter Occurrence Ranking Worksheet or a copy of the Health Professions Prestige Ranking Worksheet for each participant and for each group.

Physical Setting

Each group should be seated around a square or round table, far enough away from other groups to be able to work without distractions. Lapboards may be used.

Process

I. The facilitator distributes copies of either the Letter Occurrence Ranking Worksheet or the Health Professions Prestige Ranking Worksheet to all participants. (All receive the same form.) He directs them to rank the items according to instructions on the form that he has selected. (The facilitator may read the instructions aloud.) Participants are instructed to work independently and are given ten minutes to complete the ranking.

II. Groups are formed, and one copy of the worksheet used in step I is given to each group. Members are told to develop a group consensus on the rank to be assigned to each item. The following ground rules are presented:
  1. An individual is not to change any answers on his first worksheet as a result of the group decision.

2. One member of the group is to record the consensus decision on the group's worksheet.
3. The group has thirty minutes to complete its ranking.
4. Group members must substantially agree on the ranking of each item.
5. Averaging, majority-rule voting, and the making of "deals" are to be avoided.

III. The facilitator announces (and may post) the "correct" answers. Participants score their individual worksheets by adding the differences between their ranks and the "correct" ranks (all differences are made positive and added together). The lower the score, the closer it is to the rankings on the key. One member from each group also computes the group's score from the consensus worksheet.

IV. Each group then computes the average score of its individual members and compares this with the group's score. Groups are brought together to publish outcomes. Summary statistics from each group are posted on a chart such as the following:

Outcome	Group 1	Group 2	Group 3
Range of Individual Scores			
Average of Individual Scores			
Score for Group Consensus			
Increment for Consensus Seeking			
Synergy*	Yes No	Yes No	Yes No

*In this context, synergy is defined as the consensus score being lower than the lowest individual score in the group.

Structured Experience 157

V. The implications of the experience are then discussed, with emphasis on such points as:

    1. What form did the group discussion take? What helped consensus seeking? What hindered it?

    2. What kind of leadership emerged? How did members influence the group?

    3. How did the group discover and use information resources? Did any members reserve private information such as the layout of typewriter keys, the relative simplicity of symbols in the Morse Code, etc.?

    4. How were disagreements resolved, compromises achieved, decisions made?

    5. How do the individual members feel about the process and outcomes?

Variations

See *Volume IV*, Structured Experience 115, for variations.

Answer Keys

I. Letter Occurrence*

1.	E	9.	H
2.	T	10.	D
3.	A	11.	L
4.	O	12.	F
5.	N	13.	C
6.	R	14.	M
7.	I	15.	U
8.	S		

II. Health Professions Prestige**

1.	neurosurgeon	9.	dentist
2.	cardiologist	10.	registered nurse
3.	ophthalmologist	11.	pharmacist
4.	plastic surgeon	12.	physical therapist
5.	orthopedic surgeon	13.	osteopath
6.	pediatrician	14.	practical nurse
7.	psychiatrist	15.	chiropractor
8.	dermatologist		

---

*Based on material in A. E. Karbowiak and R. M. Huey, *Information, Computers, Machines, and Man,* New York: John Wiley, 1971.

**Adapted from S. M. Shortell, "Occupational Prestige Differences Within the Medical and Allied Health Professions," *Social Science and Medicine,* 1974, 8, 1-9.

Similar Structured Experiences: *Vol. I:* Structured Experiences **11, 15;** *Vol. II:* **30;** *Vol. III:* **64;** *'72 Annual:* **84;** *Vol. IV:* **115;** *'75 Annual:* **140;** *Vol. V:* **151, 155.**

Lecturette Source: *'73 Annual:* "Synergy and Consensus-Seeking."

Notes on the Use of "Letter Occurrence/Health Professions Prestige":

"Letter Occurrence" submitted by Kenneth D. Scott. "Health Professions Prestige" submitted by J. William Pfeiffer.

Structured Experience 157

LETTER OCCURRENCE RANKING WORKSHEET

Instructions: Below is a list of the fifteen letters that occur most often in written English. Your task is to rank these letters in the same order as their actual frequency of occurrence. Place the number *1* by the letter that you think is most frequently used, place the number 2 by the second most frequently occurring letter, and continue through number *15*, which is your estimate of the letter used least frequently.

_____	N	_____	F
_____	T	_____	I
_____	S	_____	R
_____	D	_____	H
_____	U	_____	M
_____	L	_____	A
_____	E	_____	O
_____	C		

HEALTH PROFESSIONS PRESTIGE RANKING WORKSHEET

Instructions: Below is a list of fifteen professionals in the health field. Your task is to rank these occupations according to their prestige in the United States today. Place the number *1* by the most prestigious, place the number 2 by the second most prestigious, and so on.

_____	cardiologist	_____	pediatrician
_____	chiropractor	_____	pharmacist
_____	dentist	_____	physical therapist
_____	dermatologist	_____	plastic surgeon
_____	neurosurgeon	_____	practical nurse
_____	ophthalmologist	_____	psychiatrist
_____	orthopedic surgeon	_____	registered nurse
_____	osteopath		

158. ABSENTEE: A MANAGEMENT ROLE PLAY

Goals

I. To explore the dynamics of decision making.

II. To study the resolution and management of conflict.

III. To reveal loyalty patterns among peers and superiors.

Group Size

Two groups of five to seven members each. Several pairs of groups may be directed simultaneously.

Time Required

Approximately one and one-half hours.

Materials

I. A copy of the Absentee Information Sheet for each participant.

II. A pencil and paper for each participant.

Physical Setting

A room large enough for each group to sit in a circle without distracting the other group.

Process

I. In a brief introduction, the facilitator gives an overview of the activity. He does not state the goals of the activity.

II. The facilitator forms two groups of five to seven members each. He announces that each group is to sit in a circle away from the other group. One group is designated "top management" and the other "middle management."

III. The facilitator distributes the Absentee Information Sheet to all participants and tells them to spend ten minutes studying it and making notes on how they would resolve the problem.

IV. The facilitator then tells the groups that they have twenty-five minutes to discuss the problem and to reach consensus on a solution. After the groups have been working for ten minutes, the facilitator interrupts and randomly appoints one member of each group to be its leader for the remainder of the time.

V. At the end of twenty-five minutes, the facilitator stops the discussion. He directs the middle-management leader to assume the role of spokesman for his group.

VI. The spokesman goes to the top-management group and presents the recommendations of his team. The remaining middle managers silently observe this meeting.

VII. The middle-management group is instructed to reconvene in its original meeting place to give its leader feedback and to speculate on the pending decisions of top management. Concurrently, the top-management team makes its final decision. (Five minutes.)

VIII. The top-management team summons the middle-management spokesman to receive its decision. (The other middle-management members continue their meeting.)

IX. The middle-management spokesman returns to his group to announce the decision of top management. The top-management members observe the reactions of the middle-management group and discuss their observations. (Ten minutes.)

X. Participants pair off with members of the other group to discuss their learnings. (Ten minutes.)

XI. The facilitator leads a discussion of the outcomes of the experience. He keeps the discussion from stressing the "correct" solution and focuses instead on the process.

Variations

I. The pairs of groups can be designated "labor" and "management."

II. Another problem can be used.

III. After step IX, an image exchange can be held (*Vol. III:* Structured Experience 68).

IV. A person can be designated to play the role of Novak and to attend the middle-management meetings.

Similar Structured Experiences: *Vol. III:* Structured Experience **68**; *'75 Annual:* **144, 145.**

Suggested Instruments: *'72 Annual:* "Supervisory Attitudes: The X-Y Scale"; *'73 Annual:* "LEAD (Leadership: Employee-Orientation and Differentiation) Questionnaire"; *'75 Annual:* "Problem-Analysis Questionnaire," "Decision-Style Inventory," "Diagnosing Organization Ideology."

Lecturette Sources: *'74 Annual:* "Conflict-Resolution Strategies," "Personal and Organizational Pain: Costs and Profits," "Communication Patterns in Organization Structure," "Individual Needs and Organizational Goals: An Experiential Lecture; *'75 Annual:* "Participatory Management: A New Morality," "The Supervisor as Counselor."

Notes on the Use of "Absentee":

Submitted by Richard J. Carpenter, Jr. Reprinted from *The Air Force ROTC Educational Journal* by permission of the author.

Structured Experience 158

ABSENTEE INFORMATION SHEET

Background

Bob Ford has been a test supervisor in the quality-control section for five months. He was promoted on the basis of his excellent performance in the research and development (R & D) section. Although his new subordinates do not question Ford's engineering ability, they are still grumbling about the fact that their fellow worker, Bill Novak, was passed over in favor of an "outsider."

The Critical Incidents

1. Ford's supervisor had asked to have a "good man" sent over to R & D to help out with a special problem for four days. Looking over the job and surveying his staff, Ford decided that Novak was best qualified.

   Friday afternoon, Ford called Novak into his office and said, "Bill, the superintendent has a special project going in the R & D section and needs some help. Since our schedule is flexible, I'm sending you over there for a short time; starting Monday."

   Novak answered, "Why pick me? I like the work I'm doing here. Do you have any complaints about my work?"

   Ford shook his head. "No, but I don't have time to argue with you. Be over there Monday morning."

   Novak stormed out of Ford's office without saying a word.

2. Late Monday morning, the superintendent called Ford. "I thought you were sending Novak over here to help me out. I'm on a tight schedule with a subcontractor, Bob, and I need Novak now!"

   Ford replied, "I told him to report to you this morning. He hasn't shown up here, and he should have called in by 9 o'clock if he wasn't coming in today. I assumed he was over there working with you. I'll send one of the other men over in a few minutes."

   As Ford picked up the phone to call Novak's home, his secretary walked in and announced that Novak's wife had just called. "She says Novak is sick and will probably be out for a few days."

3. Wednesday morning, Ford was holding a staff meeting; he had to leave to answer a telephone call. Returning to the conference room, he was just in time to hear one of his men, whose back was turned to him, say, "Novak really made a pile on that poker game last night, didn't he?"

   For the rest of the meeting, the men avoided Ford's glances. On Friday, Novak handed in a doctor's certificate for four days' sick leave.

   Ford knows that the crew is waiting to see what he will do.

159. FORK-LABYRINTH: LEADERSHIP PRACTICE

Goals

I. To diagnose the behavior of leaders and followers in a small group performing a complex competitive task.

II. To teach "on-line" feedback and coaching on leadership behavior.

III. To practice different leadership behaviors.

Group Size

At least two seven-person clusters.

Time Required

Approximately three hours. Additional diagnosis time can be allotted up to a full-day workshop.

Materials

I. One Fork-Labyrinth* for each seven-person cluster. This device is a 12″ × 12″ board on which several drilled holes, numbered from one to eighty, are outlined by a printed maze path. The set also contains two wire forks, placed so as to intersect each other on the board. One small steel ball is to be cradled by the forks.

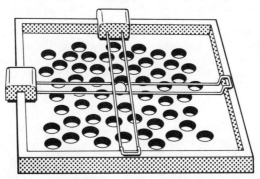

II. Two blindfolds for each cluster.

---

*Produced by BRIO of Sweden. May be purchased in major department stores or from BRIO, S-283 00, Osby, Sweden. (Approximately $20.00.)

III. A copy of the Fork-Labyrinth Task Sheet for each participant.

IV. A copy of the Fork-Labyrinth Score Sheet for each cluster.

Physical Setting

A room with a separate table for each cluster.

Process

I. The facilitator distributes a copy of the Fork-Labyrinth Task Sheet to each participant to read. He clarifies the scoring process.

II. The facilitator divides participants into clusters of seven persons each. Within each cluster, three persons are designated company A, three company B, and one scorekeeper. The facilitator stresses that A companies are in competition only with other A companies, and B companies are in competition only with B companies. He distributes a copy of the Fork-Labyrinth Score Sheet to each scorekeeper. The facilitator issues two blindfolds to each cluster.

III. Each A company selects one of its members to be the first manager, and he in turn selects two members from the B company to be his workers. He blindfolds his workers. The remaining members assume the roles of coaches/observers.

IV. The facilitator distributes the Fork-Labyrinths, checking to see that the forks run smoothly on the boards. He informs the participants that if the fork is held too tightly against the board, it will be difficult to move.

V. The manager of company A leads his workers through three rounds of the task (one set). Before and after each round, he is coached by the other members of his company and (if desirable) is encouraged to practice new or modified leadership behaviors. Simultaneously, the company-B workers receive feedback from the other members of their company. The scorekeeper records the data for each round.

VI. Steps III and V are alternated between company A and company B until all six participants have served as manager.

VII. As each cluster completes its six sets, it is instructed to discuss the leadership and follower behaviors that emerged during the experience.

VIII. The facilitator gathers the final scores and announces the winning teams from the A companies and the B companies.

IX. The facilitator then leads a discussion to process the experience. The experience focuses on the situational or contingency approach to leadership. There are enough variations in leadership style, in follower abilities, and in needs and motives to provide ample discussion of the factors involved in the "act of managing." Even the task can be viewed as shifting as the leader directs his subordinates, selects them, promotes them, and sets goals with them. The facilitator may pose the following questions:

1. Which style(s) seemed most effective, i.e., which leadership styles seemed to work best with which follower styles?
2. Did workers notice any changes in leaders' approaches? If so, what did they perceive and was it useful?
3. What are the roles of a leader and his followers in goal setting and task performance?
4. What criteria did the leader use in selecting his assistant? What changes in behavior occurred as a result of the assistant's promotion?

Variations

I. If competition between an A company and a B company is stressed, the experience becomes an intergroup-conflict experience with emphasis being placed on labor/management disputes—especially the 70/30 earnings mix.

II. Processing can be conducted at the end of set III, allowing the remaining managers to take advantage of the insights gained.

Fork-Labyrinth Normative Data

Earnings for Company A & Company B

Group	N	Average Total	Highest Total	Lowest Total	Best Total Earnings (3-Round Set)
Full-Time MBA's	60	239	367	130	107
Managers	35	234	341	103	108
Educational Administrators	30	152	229	101	63
Savings and Loan Managers	40	153	180	117	75

Round	Highest Goal Set	Highest Score Earned
1	70	35
2	45	30
3	66	65

Structured Experience 159

Similar Structured Experiences: *Vol. I:* Structured Experience **3**; *Vol. V:* **154, 162.**

Suggested Instruments: *'73 Annual:* "LEAD (Leadership: Employee-Orientation and Differentiation) Questionnaire"; *'75 Annual:* "Decision-Style Inventory."

Lecturette Sources: *'74 Annual:* "Individual Needs and Organizational Goals: An Experiential Lecture"; *'75 Annual:* "The Supervisor as Counselor."

Notes on the Use of "Fork-Labyrinth":

Submitted by John F. Veiga.

FORK-LABYRINTH TASK SHEET

In this experience, A companies will be in competition with each other and B companies will be in competition with each other. During the process, the A companies will be paired with the B companies. The A companies will provide workers for the B-company's managers to lead, and vice versa. An A-company manager will lead for three rounds, then a B-company manager will lead for three rounds, and so on in rotation until three managers from each company have participated.

The Task: The manager will lead two workers, who will attempt to negotiate the maze of a labyrinth board. Before workers begin their first round, they will put on blindfolds and will *not* remove them until the conclusion of round 3. Each worker will attempt to move one fork over the labyrinth in cooperation with another worker while both are blindfolded.

Each worker is permitted to use only *one* hand in moving the fork; the other hand may rest on the board but may *not* touch the fork. Round 1 will last five minutes, and rounds 2 and 3 will last three minutes each. *No practicing is allowed.*

Goal Setting and Scoring: At the start of each round, the manager will indicate his goal to the scorekeeper. The goal can range from 1 to 80. These numbers correspond to those printed on the path outlined on the labyrinth board.

The score depends on whether or not the goal is reached on the path without the steel ball falling into a hole. If the goal is reached, the score will be equal to the goal. If the ball falls before the goal is reached, the score is zero. If the goal is exceeded, the score still remains equal to the goal *unless* the ball falls into a hole—then the score is zero.

Outcome	Score
Goal not reached	0
Goal reached	Equal to goal
Goal exceeded without ball falling into hole	Equal to goal
Goal exceeded with ball falling into hole	0

If the manager is successful in attaining his goal, his company will receive 70 percent of the score and the workers' company will receive 30 percent of the score.

Personnel Selection: Each manager will select his two workers from the other company. The two workers selected will remain the *same* for *all* three rounds. At least one of these workers must be someone who has not been a worker in his company's previous three-round set.

Structured Experience 159

Promotion: After the second round, the manager must promote one of the two workers to be his assistant by having that person remove his blindfold before working in round 3.

Coaching: Between rounds, company members are encouraged to "coach" their teammate on his leadership style, in order to improve their score.

Winners: Winners for the most effective A and B companies will be announced after the task is completed.

FORK-LABYRINTH SCORE SHEET

As scorekeeper, you have five responsibilities:

1. To make decisions on scores.
2. To record the scores.
3. To time each round in each set.
4. To reset the board after each round.
5. To direct the unblindfolding after each round 2.

	Round 1 (Five minutes)			Round 2 (Three minutes)			Round 3 (Three minutes)			Points for set (A)	Points for set (B)
	Goal	Score	Payoff 70/30	Goal	Score	Payoff 70/30	Goal	Score	Payoff 70/30		
Set I Mgr. (A)											
Wkrs. (B)											
Set II Mgr. (B)											
Wkrs. (A)											
Set III Mgr. (A)											
Wkrs. (B)											
Set IV Mgr. (B)											
Wkrs. (A)											
Set V Mgr. (A)											
Wkrs. (B)											
Set VI Mgr. (B)											
Wkrs. (A)											

TOTAL EARNINGS _____ _____

Structured Experience 159

160. TINKERTOY BRIDGE: INTERGROUP COMPETITION

Goals

I. To analyze individual and team actions in relation to on-the-job experiences.

II. To build awareness of the need for teamwork in completing a task.

III. To demonstrate the effects of competition on team efforts.

Group Size

A minimum of twelve participants.

Time Required

Approximately one and one-half hours.

Materials

I. A box of "Junior Architect" Tinkertoys for each team.

II. A copy of the Tinkertoy Bridge General Instruction Sheet for each participant.

III. A copy of each of the following for each observer:
1. Tinkertoy Bridge Observer Sheet: Designing/Constructing.
2. Tinkertoy Bridge Observer Sheet: Organizing/Constructing.

IV. A copy of each of the following for the designers from each team:
1. Tinkertoy Bridge Design Instruction Sheet
2. Tinkertoy Bridge Template (see Directions for Making a Tinkertoy Bridge Template)
3. Tinkertoy Bridge Design Sheet.

V. A copy of the Tinkertoy Bridge Construction Instruction Sheet for each construction worker.

VI. A watch with a second hand for each observer.

VII. Newsprint, masking tape, and a felt-tipped marker.

VIII. A four-pound weight (may be made out of sand, metal, books, etc.).

Physical Setting

A room large enough for two teams to work separately without distracting each other. A separate room for each team's designers.

Process

I. The facilitator briefly introduces the activity, explaining that participants will be involved in carrying out a specific task within a team effort and in providing feedback on the process. The facilitator gives a Tinkertoy Bridge General Instruction Sheet to each participant. He emphasizes the following:

   1. Designers may not participate in the actual construction of the model. They may, however, observe and redesign if necessary.
   2. Construction workers may use only one hand to construct the model. They must follow the design on the Tinkertoy Bridge Design Sheet and must ask the designers to alter it if necessary.

II. The facilitator selects four observers. He instructs the remaining participants to divide into two equal-sized groups while he is privately briefing the observers.

III. The facilitator meets with the observers in a separate room. He gives a copy of the Tinkertoy Bridge Observer Sheet: Designing/Constructing to two of the observers and a copy of the Tinkertoy Bridge Observer Sheet: Organizing/Constructing to the other two observers. He explains their time-keeping and rule-enforcing responsibilities. Each observer must have a watch with a second hand. (During the construction phase, one observer will keep time while the other enforces rules.) The facilitator designates which team each observer will monitor. The observers and the facilitator rejoin the other participants.

IV. The facilitator directs each team to select two members to be "designers" and two members to be "construction workers." (The observers begin their tasks.)

V. The facilitator distributes a copy each of the Tinkertoy Bridge Design Instruction Sheet, the Tinkertoy Bridge Template, and the Tinkertoy Bridge Design Sheet to each set of designers. He ensures that they understand their task. He directs the two design teams and their observers to their work rooms and tells the designers that they have approximately ten minutes to complete their design.

VI. The facilitator distributes a copy of the Tinkertoy Bridge Construction Instruction Sheet and a box of Tinkertoys to the construction workers from each team. He ensures that they understand their task and directs them and their observers to their respective work areas to begin the organizing phase. He tells them that they have approximately ten minutes for this phase.

VII. Designers from each team return to the main room as soon as they have completed their design and estimates. Construction begins and designers are reminded that they may not participate physically in the construction.

VIII. Upon completion of construction, the facilitator tests each bridge by comparing it to the model and by hanging a four-pound weight at its center.

Structured Experience 160

IX. Results of each team's project are posted on newsprint. A chart such as the following may be used:

Factor	Team I		Team II	
	Estimated	Actual	Estimated	Actual
1. Material	$_____	$_____	$_____	$_____
2. Design Time	-----	_____min.	-----	_____min.
3. Design ($600 per minute)	-----	$_____	-----	$_____
4. Construction Time	_____min.	_____min.	_____min.	_____min.
5. Construction Labor ($3,000 per minute for estimated time)	$_____	$_____	$_____	$_____
6. Penalty Charges ($6,000 per minute over or under estimate)	-----	$_____	-----	$_____
7. Total Time (items 2 + 4)	_____min.	_____min.	_____min.	_____min.
8. Total Cost (items 1 + 3 + 5 + 6)	$_____	$_____	$_____	$_____

X. Each team gives a two-minute report to the observers on "who should be awarded the contract and why."

XI. The observers decide publicly which team is to be awarded the contract. Participants discuss their "feeling" reactions to the decision.

XII. Each observer meets with his team and critiques it. Teams then critique themselves and discuss specific actions they could have taken to operate more effectively as a team. (Fifteen minutes.)

XIII. The facilitator leads a discussion of how the experience compares with real jobs in work situations. He encourages the participants to be as specific as possible. He directs them to focus on the ways in which the activity compares with operations, conflicts, teamwork, etc., in actual work situations.

Variations

    I. Another construction project, with other materials, may be used.

    II. Supplies may be "purchased" (see Structured Experience 161 in this volume).

    III. The designing and constructing tasks can be done by the same persons.

    IV. To accelerate the process, a blueprint may be furnished to each team.

Similar Structured Experiences: *Vol. II:* Structured Experiences **29, 32;** *Vol. III:* **54;** *'72 Annual:* **78, 81;** *Vol. IV:* **105;** *Vol. V:* **161, 163.**
Lecturette Source: *'73 Annual:* "Win/Lose Situations."

Notes on the Use of "Tinkertoy Bridge":

Submitted by Geoff Bellman.

Structured Experience 160

TINKERTOY BRIDGE GENERAL INSTRUCTION SHEET

The State Highway Department has asked your company to design and construct a model of a new bridge across the Mandan River. Other companies are also designing bridges for other locations. The highway department is going to have twenty bridges built around the state, and will award a contract for all the remaining bridges to one of the companies. All the competing companies are building models. You want your company's model to win.

The highway department will make its decision based on a number of factors, including:

Strength—If the model will support a weight of four pounds at its center, it will meet the state's minimum standards.

Actual vs. Contract Cost, Actual vs. Contract Time—Being close to contract cost and time is to your advantage.

Low Cost—This is naturally an important consideration. Cost figures will be available to your designers.

There are two main tasks facing your company:

1. Drawing the design
2. Constructing the model.

Designers will be given a design sheet and specific design instructions. Construction workers will be given instructions and adequate building materials.

TINKERTOY BRIDGE OBSERVER SHEET: DESIGNING/CONSTRUCTING

Design Phase

How were the designers selected? Were their abilities considered?

How did the designers divide the work to be done?

Who influenced decisions the most? How?

Did the designers see themselves as part of a team with the construction workers? How did they show this?

What happened among the designers that caused them to use their time well? Poorly?

How much attention did they pay to bridge standards (strength, materials, and labor costs)? How much time did they spend deciding costs?

Construction Phase

What did the construction workers do when they first began construction?

Did the construction workers follow the plans and organizations that they set up earlier?

Structured Experience 160

Did these work?

Did the construction workers follow the Tinkertoy Bridge Design Sheet in actually building the bridge?

Did they build subassemblies?

Did they cooperate well in the actual construction phase?

Did the construction workers have any problems with the design? How were the problems handled?

Did the construction workers see their designers as friends or as enemies? How was this shown?

How did the construction workers use the designers' ideas during construction? How was the design changed? Who suggested the change?

How realistic were the material and labor cost estimates? How could they have been improved?

What happened if the model did not meet the strength specifications?

TINKERTOY BRIDGE OBSERVER SHEET: ORGANIZING/CONSTRUCTING

Organizing Phase

How were the construction workers selected? Were their abilities considered?

What did the construction workers do while the designers were designing?

Did the construction workers organize themselves? How?

Did they sort materials?

Did they assign jobs?

Did they practice assembly?

Did they plan how they would build the bridge?

What else did they do?

How did the construction workers feel about the designers? Did they see them as team-mates? Why or why not?

Were the construction workers oriented toward the designers' objectives? Why or why not?

Structured Experience 160

Construction Phase

What did the construction workers do when they first began construction?

Did the construction workers follow the plans and organization that they set up earlier? Did these work?

Did the construction workers follow the Tinkertoy Bridge Design Sheet in actually building the bridge?

Did they build subassemblies?

Did they cooperate well in the actual construction phase?

Did the construction workers have any problems with the design? How were the problems handled?

Did the construction workers see their designers as friends or as enemies? How was this shown?

How realistic were the material and labor cost estimates? How could they have been improved?

What happened if the model did not meet the strength specifications?

How did the construction workers use the designers' ideas during construction? How was the design changed? Who suggested the change?

TINKERTOY BRIDGE DESIGN INSTRUCTION SHEET

Design a model bridge with a minimum length of AB (points on the design sheet) and a minimum width of AC that *will support a weight of four pounds at its center.*

You have been given:

1. A blank design sheet

2. A template for drawing.

The design, with at least two views completed,* must be finished—along with cost estimates—before you take it to the construction workers.

There are four cost factors:

1. Design time costs $600 per minute.

2. Straight-time construction labor costs $3,000 per minute for every minute of estimated time. (Put your estimated time on the design sheet.)

3. Penalty charges cost $6,000 per minute for every minute of actual construction time above or below the estimated time.

4. Materials cost from $100 to $600 each. (Amounts are listed on the template; put your estimated cost on the design sheet.)

Each construction worker may use only one hand during the construction. *Construction workers cannot design and designers cannot build.*

Two members of each team will be selected to be designers. The rest of the team will be construction workers. The design will be prepared in another room. Construction will be in this room.

---

*The design should be clear to the construction workers, but exactness is not necessary.

DIRECTIONS FOR MAKING A TINKERTOY BRIDGE TEMPLATE

To the facilitator:

This template is to be made of cardboard. (Shaded areas are to be cut out.) It is to be presented to the designers for their use in drawing the design for their team's bridge. The pieces of the template must be drawn to scale.

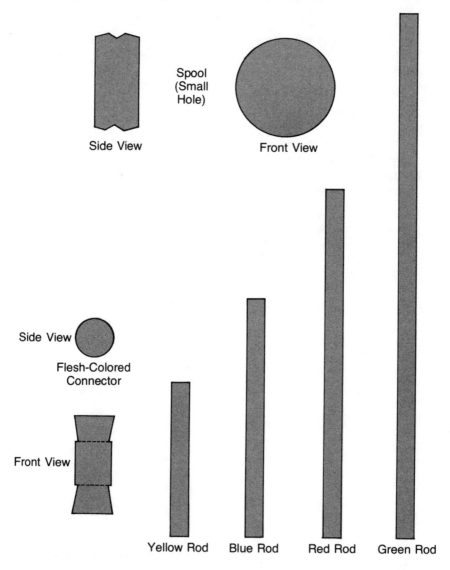

Construction Piece	Inventory	Cost per Piece
Spool	20	$200
Connector	8	$100
Rod, yellow	12	$300
Rod, blue	12	$400
Rod, red	10	$500
Rod, green	10	$600

TINKERTOY BRIDGE CONSTRUCTION INSTRUCTION SHEET

You will be building a model bridge out of the materials given to you. The design for this bridge will also be given to you. You may not begin assembling the model bridge until construction time begins. The model must be able to support a four-pound weight at its center.

Remember: *During construction you may use only one hand.*

Follow the design, but if you feel that it will not work, is not strong enough, or is too expensive or time consuming, you may ask the designers to change it. (They *may not* change the material and labor cost estimates but they may change the design itself.) You are not finished until the design and the model match.

Structured Experience 160

TINKERTOY BRIDGE DESIGN SHEET

To the facilitator:

This sheet is to be reproduced on 30" x 34" paper (two sheets of newsprint can be used). Designers are to draw their bridge design to scale, using the Tinkertoy Bridge Template.

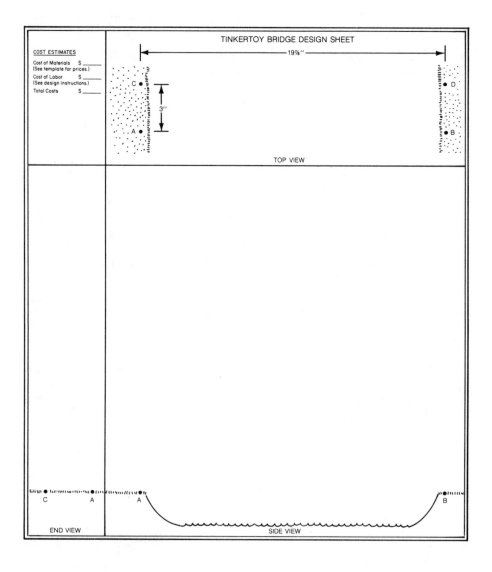

161. LEGO BRIDGE:
INTERGROUP COMPETITION

Goals

    I. To observe spontaneous patterns of organization in work groups.

    II. To explore the relationship between planning and production.

    III. To study the effects of intergroup competition on team functioning.

Group Size

    An unlimited number of groups of from five to eight members each.

Time Required

    Approximately one and one-half hours.

Materials

    I. A copy of the Lego Bridge Information Sheet for each group.

    II. At least 200 Lego blocks for each group.

    III. One complete set of spans for each group. Spans can be made from any sturdy material (wood, masonite, etc.) and are to be 100 mm wide. The lengths of the six spans are as follows: 450, 460, 470, 480, 490, and 500 mm.

    IV. Newsprint, felt-tipped markers, and masking tape.

    V. A metric ruler for each group.

    VI. Paper and pencils for each group.

Physical Setting

    A room large enough to permit groups to work without being distracted or influenced by other groups. Alternatively, one room could be used during the introductory and processing phases, with smaller individual rooms used by the groups during the problem-solving phase.

Process

    I. The facilitator divides the participants into groups of five to eight members each.

Each group then designates one of its members to function solely as process observer.

II. The facilitator distributes a copy of the Lego Bridge Information Sheet to each participant.

III. After the participants have read the Lego Bridge Information Sheet, the facilitator distributes two hundred Lego blocks, a metric ruler, paper, and pencils to each group. He reminds the groups that they are not to submit a bid for the bridge, but are to predict their profit.

IV. The facilitator announces the start of the forty-minute design and profit-predicting time. He takes note of the time.

V. When thirty-five minutes have passed, the facilitator announces the time; at the end of forty minutes, he calls time. He then collects and posts the profit expectations and span length for each group.

VI. The facilitator gives each team a span the length of its bridge design. He collects all blocks that have not been "purchased" and reminds the participants that each assembly second is worth $3,333. He also answers any procedural questions.

VII. The facilitator announces the beginning of the construction phase. He takes note of the time.

VIII. After the construction phase is completed, each group prepares a profit and loss statement and submits it to the facilitator.

IX. Each team is directed to prepare a report on how it would improve its process if it could do the task again. The observers lead this process. (Fifteen minutes.) During this time, the facilitator checks the accuracy of each profit and loss statement.

X. The facilitator directs the teams to present their reports; he then leads a discussion of the experience, which includes how the group processed ideas and how it disciplined itself.

XI. The facilitator posts a summary of the profit and loss statements and announces the winner.

Variations

I. The building materials can be varied.

II. Pairs of tables can be set to simulate the banks on either side of a river. The bridge construction spans the space between the two tables.

III. Teams can be penalized for inaccurate time estimates. The cost per minute can be increased for time in excess of the team's prediction.

IV. Several participants can be assigned timing, policing, and observing roles.

V. Each team can be divided into two functional units: planning and construction.

VI. The same general design can be used with a different product.

Similar Structured Experiences: *Vol. II:* Structured Experiences **29, 32;** *Vol. III:* **54;** *'72 Annual:* **78, 81;** *Vol. IV:* **105;** *Vol. V:* **160, 163.**
Lecturette Source: *'73 Annual:* "Win/Lose Situations."

Notes on the Use of "Lego Bridge":

Submitted by Peter Mumford, with acknowledgement to the Reed Paper Group Ltd. Reprinted by permission from *Canadian Training Methods*, April 1, 1974, pp. 24–25.

Structured Experience 161

LEGO BRIDGE INFORMATION SHEET

Your Group's Task

You are a project team employed by Bridge Builders, Inc. You have contracted to build a bridge over the Indian River between Old Bankstown and New Bankstown. The bridge is needed because the previous bridge collapsed. The Indian River is a raging torrent, 450 mm wide at the point where the collapse occurred. Engineering studies indicate that the major cause of failure was the total unsuitability of the river bed for any sort of supporting pier for a bridge. All future bridges, therefore, must be single-span structures.

You are to advise the facilitator on design (including the desired span length) and on the expected profit to the company.

Stage 1: Planning

You have forty minutes in which to conduct your evaluation of the situation. At the end of this time, your group will be asked to announce its profit expectation. At this point also, any materials not called for in the design will be collected. You may use the remaining materials to test your design but may not prefabricate any parts of the design to assist stage 2.

Stage 2: Construction

You will be provided with the materials called for in your design. Your construction time will be measured precisely.

Contract Terms

Span (mm)	Required Height (mm)	Payment
450	100	$3,000,000
460	110	$3,100,000
470	120	$3,250,000
480	130	$3,500,000
490	140	$3,800,000
500	150	$4,100,000

There must be a ramp at each end of the span. These ramps must be at least as wide as the span.

Diagram

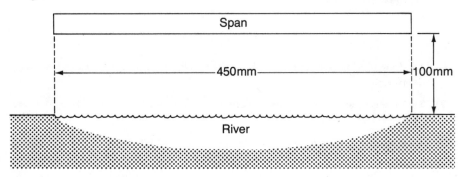

Cost Factors

Land: Donated by the Indian River Bridge Authority.

Span: Contracted by a different firm (no charges to your company).

Labor and overhead: $200,000 per minute of construction.

Building materials: $10,000 for each Lego block, regardless of size, when the initial purchase is made prior to construction. After the construction stage begins, the price per block will be $12,000. Unused blocks can be returned to the supplier for a refund at the rate of $5,000 per block.

162. PINS AND STRAWS: LEADERSHIP STYLES

Goals

I. To dramatize three general styles of leadership: autocratic, laissez-faire, and democratic.

II. To increase awareness of how different styles of leadership can affect the performance of subordinates.

III. To study the phenomenon of competition among groups.

Group Size

An unlimited number of groups of six members each. The example is based on at least six groups.

Time Required

Approximately two hours.

Materials

I. One package of drinking straws (100 per package) for each group.

II. One package of straight pins for each group.

III. A copy of one strip from the Pins and Straws Leaders Instructions Sheet (cut into strips to separate the three variations) for each group leader.

IV. A copy of the Pins and Straws Observer Worksheet for each process observer.

V. A copy of the Pins and Straws Discussion Sheet for each participant.

VI. Newsprint, felt-tipped markers, and masking tape.

VII. Paper and a pencil for each participant.

Physical Setting

One large room for the initial and final meetings of all participants, with a large table on which to display the straw structure. It is desirable to provide a separate room for each group to work independently on its structure.

Process

    I. The facilitator forms groups of six persons each.

    II. One participant within each group is selected to be an observer. The facilitator distributes a copy of the Pins and Straws Observer Worksheet to each of the observers.

    III. One participant within each group is selected to be the leader. The leaders are instructed to assemble privately with the facilitator to receive instructions and materials.

    IV. The facilitator briefs the leaders on the task, distributes pins and straws to each group, and gives each leader a strip from the Pins and Straws Leaders Instructions Sheet. They are reminded to follow their instructions explicitly, and not to show their strips to anyone. (Since there are three *different* sets of instructions—autocratic, laissez-faire, and democratic—the facilitator distributes the instruction strips so that there will be an approximately equal number of leaders [at least two] with each of the different kinds of instructions. It will aid the facilitator in recording the data at the conclusion of the experience if he writes group numbers on the Pins and Straws Leaders Instructions Sheets so that the same instructions occur in consecutive order. For example, if there are six groups, group *one* receives *democratic* instructions, group *two* receives *democratic* instructions, group *three* receives *autocratic* instructions, group *four* receives *autocratic* instructions, group *five* receives *laissez-faire* instructions, and group *six* receives *laissez-faire* instructions, etc.)

    V. The facilitator announces that the task of each group is to build a structure out of pins and straws. Fifteen minutes will be allowed for this task. Afterward, the structures will be "judged" on the equal bases of height, strength, and beauty.

    VI. At the end of the construction phase, the facilitator instructs participants to rate their experience in the group on three dimensions. They are to use a five-point scale (5 is high). The dimensions are:
        1. Satisfaction with the leader
        2. Satisfaction with your participation
        3. Satisfaction with the group's product.
The facilitator directs each group to compute its members' average for each of the three dimensions.

    VII. Groups bring their structures to a common display area.

    VIII. The facilitator calls for the average ratings of each group and posts them on a chart such as the following.

Structured Experience 162

Group	Average Ratings			Voting Tally			
	Leadership	Participation	Product	Height	Strength	Beauty	Total
1							
2							
3							
4							
5							
6							

IX. The facilitator directs the voting. Separate votes are held for each of the three criteria, and the numbers are tallied on the chart. Each participant may vote only once on each criterion. Voting is done by a show of hands, with eyes closed.

X. After all the data are recorded, the facilitator (a) reads aloud the instructions for each of the three styles of leadership; (b) records the description of each leader's style beside the appropriate group number; and (c) leads a discussion of the data. Some discussion guidelines are:

1. Leadership style affects group performance in complex ways. (Is there variation between the sculptures in terms of the most beautiful not being the highest or strongest, etc?)

2. One would expect an ownership bias to appear in the fact that each group votes for its own sculpture as the best in all three dimensions. Since there are an equal number of members in each group, the ownership hypothesis would predict a tie in all three votes. Yet this rarely occurs. How does this show that leadership can affect a group's feeling of ownership in a product?

3. Notice the relationship between leadership style and participation. Which leadership style utilizes the most, and which leadership style utilizes the least, resources of the group?

4. How does the brief amount of time allotted to do this task affect different leadership styles and the group's performance?

5. What is the relationship between participation and satisfaction of group members? What are the long-term and short-term implications of the relationships between leadership style and member satisfaction?

XI. The facilitator directs participants to return to their groups of six for a discussion. These discussions are led by the observers, who distribute copies of the Pins and Straws Discussion Sheet to all group members. (Thirty minutes.)

Variations

    I. Judges can be used instead of group voting.

    II. Voting can be carried out with eyes open.

    III. Other criteria, e.g., cooperation, creativity, speed, can be applied.

    IV. Other materials and another product can be used.

Similar Structured Experiences: *Vol. I:* Structured Experience 3; *Vol. V:* **154, 159.**

Suggested Instruments: *'73 Annual:* "LEAD (Leadership: Employee-Orientation and Differentiation) Questionnaire"; *'75 Annual:* Decision-Style Inventory."

Lecturette Sources: *'74 Annual:* "Individual Needs and Organizational Goals: An Experiential Lecture"; *'75 Annual:* "The Supervisor as Counselor."

Notes on the Use of "Pins and Straws":

Submitted by Howard L. Fromkin.

Structured Experience 162

PINS AND STRAWS LEADERS INSTRUCTIONS SHEET

Your job is to be as much of a dictator as you possibly can. It is important that you demonstrate this style of leadership to your group *without informing them of what you are doing.* Avoid accepting *any* suggestions from any group members. Give orders about the planning and construction. The sculpture is to be constructed from *your* ideas.

Your job is to be as much of a laissez-faire ("hands off") leader as you possibly can. It is important that you demonstrate this style of leadership to your group *without informing them of what you are doing.* Avoid making any suggestions about how or what is to be done or who is to do it. Let every group member do whatever he wants. The sculpture is to be constructed from *their* ideas.

Your job is to be as much of a democratic leader as you possibly can. It is important that you demonstrate this style of leadership to your group *without informing them of what you are doing.* When a suggestion is made by you or by any group member, ask to see how many of the group members agree with the idea. Push for some degree of consensus before any idea is acted on. The sculpture is to be the result of the *group's* ideas.

PINS AND STRAWS OBSERVER WORKSHEET

Your task is to observe the group's behavior. You do not participate. Position yourself where you can observe the behavior of all the group members.

1. Who was the group's leader?

2. Describe his leadership style. Give some examples of his behavior that illustrate that style.

3. Cite any other behaviors that you think were related to the leader's style of management. Note the member's name next to each specific behavior.

4. Describe the climate or atmosphere of the group. Give some examples of group members' behavior that illustrate this climate. Record the members' names and note their specific behavior.

5. Describe the involvement or participation of the group members in this task.

6. Cite some examples of behavior of individual members to illustrate the participation characteristics of your group. Record the members' names and note their specific behavior.

After the voting phase is completed, you will lead a thirty-minute discussion of the group's process with the members of the group. It is your responsibility to report your observations during this discussion, but avoid making a speech.

Structured Experience 162

PINS AND STRAWS DISCUSSION SHEET

Work Group

1. How did it feel to work under the leadership style of your leader?

2. How did it feel to lead with that style?

3. What are the effects of that leadership style? Advantages and disadvantages? (Use the ratings that you recorded at the end of the construction phase.)

4. Did this activity *remind* you of any effects of leadership style? What were they?

5. Did this activity demonstrate any *new* effects of leadership style? What were they?

Total Group

1. What have we learned from this activity?

2. How does what we have learned relate to our own personal styles of leadership?

3. How does what we have learned relate to our jobs back home? How can we translate what we have learned to our actions on the job?

4. Did this activity *remind* you of any effects of leadership style? What were they?

5. Did this activity demonstrate any *new* effects of leadership style? What were they?

163. COLORING BOOK:
AN ORGANIZATION EXPERIMENT

Goals

To explore relationships between organizational design and task complexity.

Group Size

A minimum of thirteen participants. (Two equal-sized groups of five to seven participants each, plus three persons to serve as judges/timekeepers/customers.)

Time Required

Approximately one and one-half hours.

Materials

I. One box of eight crayons of various colors for each participant. (Each set must contain the same array of colors.)

II. Approximately one hundred copies of the Coloring Book Cover Stock on 8½" × 11" paper for each team.

III. One copy of the Coloring Book Contract Terms Sheet for each team.

Physical Setting

A table and chairs for each group, placed so that the groups can work without distracting each other.

Process

I. The facilitator introduces the activity and states the goal.

II. He selects three participants, each of whom will serve in the multiple role of judge/timekeeper/customer. He divides the remaining participants into two teams, which are designated A and B.

III. When the teams are seated at tables, the facilitator gives a box of crayons to each team member and gives ten copies of the Coloring Book Cover Stock to each team. He explains that each team's task is to indicate the color scheme to be used on the cover of a child's coloring book. The teams are advised to consider efficiency of production as well as attractiveness of design, since the cover will later be mass produced. Each team is to prepare five identical copies of its final design. These copies are to be marked "Model, Team (A or B)." (Twenty minutes.)

IV. Each team submits five copies of its design to the judges, and the facilitator directs the judges to select one team's cover design to be used in the actual production of the cover. The judges are to make their selection on the basis of (a) aesthetic appeal and (b) ease of production.

V. While the judges make their decision, the team members process the experience in terms of:
1. How they organized themselves for the task;
2. Whether their organization was suitable to the complexity of the task and the personalities of the members.
(During the discussion, the facilitator collects the boxes of crayons and all extra copies of the cover stock.)

VI. The judges announce their decision. The facilitator states that the winning team's color designations will be used as the models for mass production of the coloring book cover.

VII. The facilitator gives one copy of the winning cover model to each team. He tells the teams that they are now in the business of producing covers for children's coloring books and that the covers must be produced in accordance with the model.

VIII. Each team receives a copy of the Coloring Book Contract Terms Sheet. The facilitator announces that the teams will be in competition to produce covers for maximum profit. The customers have placed an order with each team for six dozen units of coloring book covers, at $3.00 per dozen. These must be delivered no later than twenty minutes after the beginning of the production phase. The teams must purchase cover stock at $0.10 per piece and crayons at $1.00 per box of eight. In addition, they must compute their labor costs at $0.25 per minute or fraction thereof. The facilitator adds that there are two other factors to be considered in the cost/profit calculation:
1. The customers will buy only those covers that meet their standards of quality.
2. If the production order is not completed, the price of the covers that are produced will be reduced to $2.40 per dozen.

IX. The teams are allowed ten minutes to plan and to purchase supplies. In the meantime, the facilitator instructs the three participants who previously served as judges to act as timekeepers during the cover-production phase of the experience. Teams are instructed to place the team's initial (A or B) on the back of each cover.

X. The production phase begins. When both teams have completed their covers, or at the end of twenty minutes, the timekeepers indicate how much time each team is to be charged. The timekeepers then assume the roles of customers.

XI. The teams present their finished covers to the customers, who accept or reject each one according to whether it is an acceptable facsimile of the model. The number of acceptable covers delivered by each team is determined. While the customers are making their selections, the team members process their organization for the task in terms of its appropriateness for the nature and complexity of the task.

XII. The teams compute their sales income (based on the number of acceptable covers delivered and whether the full production price or the underproduction price was paid); they deduct costs for cover stock, crayons, and labor; and they announce their total amount of profit (or loss). The team with the greater profit wins.

XIII. The facilitator then leads all participants in a discussion of the experience. This may include the following questions: "What type of organizational design is most suited to complex, ill-defined, and nonroutine work as opposed to simple, well-defined, and routine work? Why are different organizational designs better in one situation than in the other? What are the implications for your 'back-home' organization?" This final question is emphasized by the facilitator. The expected responses will center around the fact that during the first phase the groups are decentralized, flexible, and characterized by a high degree of communication and change. In contrast, the groups in the second phase evolve into a form that is highly structured, explicitly coordinated, and relatively inflexible. Participants should become aware that the first organizations resemble *professional* organizations (or top management), characterized as dealing with complex work and varied situations, whereas the second organizational form typifies a formalized *bureaucratic* organization with routine and relatively stable work characteristics.

Variations

I. The criterion for winning can be quantity—the most covers produced in a given time—rather than profitability.

II. A bidding session can be held. The team that is not awarded a contract can observe during the production phase.

III. The product can be varied.

Similar Structured Experiences: *Vol. II:* Structured Experiences **29, 32;** *Vol. III:* **54;** *'72 Annual:* **78, 81, 82;** *Vol. IV:* **105;** *Vol. V:* **160, 161.**

Structured Experience 163

Suggested Instruments: '75 *Annual:* "Problem-Analysis Questionnaire," "Diagnosing Organization Ideology."

Lecturette Source: '75 *Annual:* "Skill Climate and Organizational Blockages."

Notes on the Use of "Coloring Book":

Based on material submitted by Michael J. Miller.

COLORING BOOK COVER STOCK

COLORING BOOK CONTRACT TERMS SHEET

Production order: Six dozen units at $3.00 per dozen ($0.25 each).
Delivery "date": No later than twenty minutes after production begins.
Underproduction penalty: Price reduced to $2.40 per dozen ($0.20 each).
Production costs: Cover stock at $0.10 each.
       Crayons at $1.00 per box of eight.
       Labor at $0.25 per minute or fraction thereof.

Accounting

 Income

  _____ Units at _____ each $ _____

 Costs

  _____ Covers at $0.10 each $ _____

  _____ Crayon sets at $1.00 each $ _____

  _____ Minutes of labor at $0.25 each $ _____

            Total costs $ _____

           Total profit (loss) $ _____

164. TESTING: INTERGROUP COMPETITION

Goals

I. To explore the impact of the lack of communication in competitive situations.

II. To demonstrate the need for collaboration and interdependence.

Group Size

An unlimited number of pairs of groups of three to seven members each. The groups should be as nearly equal in size as possible.

Time Required

Approximately one and one-half hours.

Materials

I. A copy of the Testing Score Sheet for each group.

II. A set of precut Testing Question Blanks for each group.

III. A set of precut Testing Answer Blanks for each group.

IV. A pencil for each group.

Physical Setting

A room large enough for the groups to meet without interfering with or being overheard by each other.

Process

I. The facilitator divides the participants into an even number of nearly equal-sized groups and gives each group a number designation. The groups are instructed to seat themselves apart from the other groups.

II. The facilitator explains that the activity will be a test of knowledge and strategy. He indicates that each group will design ten one-item tests for one of the other groups. The tests, which will be in each of ten assigned categories, will be distributed one at a time. Points will be awarded for correct answers. *Groups must score at least one hundred points to be eligible to win.* (The group with the highest score above one hundred wins.)

III. The facilitator pairs up groups that are physically separated from each other. He explains that these paired groups will construct the tests for each other, with each group answering the questions submitted to it by the opposite group.

IV. The facilitator distributes a copy of the Testing Score Sheet, a set of Testing Question Blanks, and a set of Testing Answer Blanks to each group. He reads the ground rules aloud and answers procedural questions.

V. The facilitator announces that each group is to discuss its strategy and formulate its first question. He also announces that ten minutes will be allowed before the first question must be distributed, but for subsequent questions only two minutes each will be allowed. Three minutes will be allowed for each answer. After ten minutes, the facilitator announces that one person from each group is to bring its question to a central location and be ready to exchange it *silently* for the question brought from its paired group. When all the questions have been carried to the center, the facilitator gives the signal for the simultaneous exchange and announces the beginning of the three-minute period in which each group will answer the question submitted to it.

VI. After three minutes, the facilitator calls for the answers to be exchanged in the same manner as were the questions.

VII. The facilitator announces that there will be two minutes to formulate the next question. Along with this question, each group is to indicate whether the previous question was answered correctly.

VIII. During each round of questions and answers, the facilitator reminds the groups of the category and point value of the question. After questions 3, 6, and 9, he allows three minutes for the group representatives (if any were chosen by the paired groups) to confer with one another in a neutral place.

IX. After round ten, the facilitator directs each group to discuss questions such as the following:
   1. What happened? How did you feel?
   2. What changes occurred in your mood?
   3. Who was the adversary in this game? What did you need to win? What did it take to lose?
   4. In what other situations do you see this happening?
   5. What factors, conditions, or circumstances made it easy to compete and hard to collaborate? Do these factors, conditions, or circumstances exist in the other situations where you see this happening?

X. The facilitator elicits comments about the process from the separate groups. The facilitator discusses win-lose, lose-lose, and win-win strategies.

XI. The facilitator calls for the final score for each group and announces a winner, if there is one.

Variations

    I. The activity can be carried out using money instead of points.

    II. Process observers can be assigned to each group.

    III. Paired groups can be placed in separate rooms, to minimize participants' breaking the rules.

Similar Structured Experiences: *Vol. II:* Structured Experiences **32, 35, 36;** *Vol. III:* **54, 61;** *'72 Annual:* **81, 82, 83;** *Vol. IV:* **105;** *'75 Annual:* **147;** *Vol. V:* **150, 160, 161, 163.**

Lecturette Sources: *'72 Annual:* "Assumptions About the Nature of Man," "McGregor's Theory X-Theory Y Model"; *'73 Annual:* "Win/Lose Situations."

Notes on the Use of "Testing":

Submitted by Peter R. Scholtes.

Structured Experience 164

TESTING SCORE SHEET

Ground Rules

1. The Testing Question Blanks and Testing Answer Blanks are to be used to transmit one paired group's question to the opposite group and to return that group's answer to the question.
2. After questions 3, 6, and 9 have been exchanged, the paired groups may select one representative each to meet together for three minutes. The representatives may discuss any topic they wish. Those groups who wish to select representatives must indicate so in the appropriate spaces on answer forms 3, 6, and 9.
3. No communication is permitted between the two groups other than the above exchange of forms and meetings through representatives.
4. No communication is permitted at all with any other groups participating in the activity.
5. Question and answer forms are to be exchanged at the same time by all groups, when so directed by the facilitator.
6. Any dispute over the fairness of a question or the correctness of an answer is to be settled by the group that formulated the question, and there is no appeal to its decision. Groups are urged, however, to make their questions clear, specific, and unequivocal. Questions may have several parts with the assigned points distributed among the different parts at the discretion of the questioning group.

Round	Topic	Points	Our Score		Their Score	
			This Round	Cumulative	This Round	Cumulative
1	Sports	10				
2	American History	10				
3*	Science	15				
4	American Politics	15				
5	Movies	15				
6*	World History	25				
7	Advertising	15				
8	U. S. Geography	15				
9*	Popular Music	30				
10	Wild Card (any topic)	50				

*After rounds 3, 6, and 9, a representative from your group may have a three-minute meeting with the representative of the other group, during which they may discuss whatever they choose.

TESTING QUESTION BLANKS

---

1. From Group _____ To Group _____

You will be informed if your answer is correct when you receive question 2.

---

2. From Group _____ To Group _____

correct.
Your answer to question 1 was incorrect.

---

3. From Group _____ To Group _____

correct.
Your answer to question 2 was incorrect.

---

4. From Group _____ To Group _____

correct.
Your answer to question 3 was incorrect.

---

5. From Group _____ To Group _____

correct.
Your answer to question 4 was incorrect.

---

6. From Group _____ To Group _____

correct.
Your answer to question 5 was incorrect.

---

7. From Group _____ To Group _____

correct.
Your answer to question 6 was incorrect.

---

8. From Group _____ To Group _____

correct.
Your answer to question 7 was incorrect.

Structured Experience 164

9. From Group _____ To Group _____

correct.
Your answer to question 8 was incorrect.

10. From Group _____ To Group _____

correct.
Your answer to question 9 was incorrect.

11. From Group _____ To Group _____

(No question.)

correct.
Your answer to question 10 was incorrect.

TESTING ANSWER BLANKS

1. From Group _____ To Group _____

2. From Group _____ To Group _____

3. From Group _____ To Group _____

do
We do not want a meeting of
representatives.

4. From Group _____ To Group _____

5. From Group _____ To Group _____

6. From Group _____ To Group _____

do
We do not want a meeting of
representatives.

7. From Group _____ To Group _____

8. From Group _____ To Group _____

9. From Group _____ To Group _____

do
We do not want a meeting of
representatives.

10. From Group _____ To Group _____

Structured Experience 164

165. MARBLES:
A COMMUNITY EXPERIMENT

Goals

I. To study community from the perspectives of establishing, enforcing, and interpreting rules.

II. To explore rule-governed behaviors.

Group Size

A minimum of ten participants.

Time Required

Approximately two hours.

Materials

I. A shooting surface.* (See Directions for Making a Marbles Shooting Surface.)

II. Marbles
1. 200 multicolored (currency)
2. 4 gold (trouble)
3. 6 green (job)
4. 10 blue (public job)
5. 10 large (protection)

III. A plastic or paper cup for each participant.

IV. A set of wooden dowel pieces ($1^{1}/_{16}$" diameter; 4", 3", 3", 2", and 1" lengths). (These should be cut evenly so that they can be stacked end on end.)

V. A three-minute egg timer.

VI. Twenty-four four-nub Lego blocks.

VII. Newsprint, felt-tipped markers, and masking tape.

VIII. Paper and a pencil for each participant.

IX. A copy of the Marbles Pre-Established-Rules Sheet for each participant.

---

*A kit with expanded rules and game materials (marbles, cups, dowels, timer, Lego blocks, printed felt, etc., but not the board and bumpers), entitled "They Shoot Marbles, Don't They?," is available from Urbex Affiliates, Inc., P.O. Box 2198, Ann Arbor, Michigan 48106. Telephone: (313) 973-2233. Cost is $40.00 plus postage.

X. One copy of the Marbles Role-Descriptions Sheet, cut into strips to separate the role descriptions.

Process

Note: Although this activity appears to be complex and does require some study, it is manageable without a great deal of preparation. The developers encourage innovation in implementing the design.

I. The facilitator discusses the goals and gives a brief overview of the activity.

II. He assigns the ten roles. (Special consideration should be given to selection of the treasurer.) More than one participant may be assigned to each of the following roles: observer, rule maker, and rule enforcer.

III. The facilitator distributes copies of the Marbles Pre-Established-Rules Sheet to all participants and answers questions to clarify the rules.

IV. He distributes the role-description strips and instructs role players to study them silently. Each player receives *only* his role strip and is not to see the role strips for the other players.

V. The facilitator announces that the first action will be taken by the treasurer, who will distribute cups and marbles to appropriate persons.

VI. Rounds 1 and 2 are carried out under the direction of the treasurer.

VII. At the end of round 2, the facilitator calls, "Time out," and directs the observer to make a brief report. No discussion is permitted.

VIII. Rounds 3 and 4 are carried out under the direction of the treasurer.

IX. The facilitator calls for a second report from the observer, as in step VII.

X. Rounds 5 and 6 are carried out under the direction of the treasurer, and a winner is announced.

XI. The facilitator calls for a final report from the observer.

XII. The facilitator directs the shooters to pair off with nonshooters. Their task is to agree on a statement about the effects of rules. (Ten minutes.)

XIII. The facilitator elicits a statement from each pair and leads a general discussion of the implications of the activity.

Structured Experience 165

Variations

I. The facilitator may "coach" the treasurer prior to the meeting, or he may play the role himself.

II. Countless variations of this structured experience are possible. The process described above includes a number of arbitrary decisions by the editors, based on suggestions in F. L. Goodman, *They Shoot Marbles, Don't They?*, Ann Arbor, Mich.: Urbex Affiliates, Inc.

Similar Structured Experiences: *Vol. III:* Structured Experience **73;** *'75 Annual:* **147.**
Suggested Instrument: *'75 Annual:* "Diagnosing Organization Ideology."
Lecturette Source: *'73 Annual:* "Win/Lose Situations."

Notes on the Use of "Marbles":

Adapted by special permission of Frederick L. Goodman and Urbex Affiliates, Inc.

DIRECTIONS FOR MAKING A MARBLES SHOOTING SURFACE

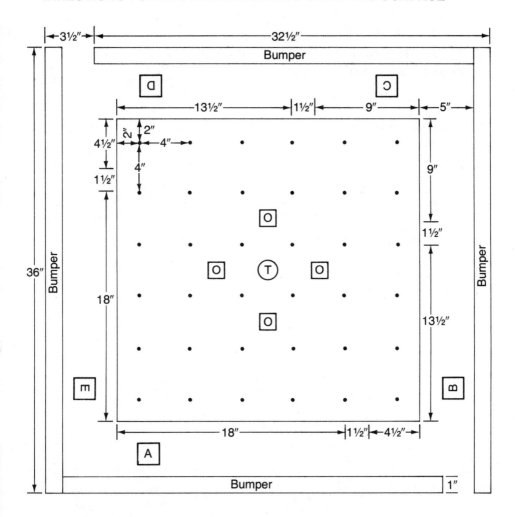

Legend

A B C D and E are seating positions for the five shooters.

O 's are positions for the "trouble marbles."

T is the position for the dowel tower.

Structured Experience 165

Materials Needed

36″ × 36″ × ¼″ plywood sheet

1″ × 2″ × 36″ side bumpers—2 pieces at opposite ends

1″ × 2″ × 32½″ side bumpers—2 pieces at opposite ends

36″ × 36″ sheet of felt

Instructions

1. Temporarily tack the felt covering to the board, making sure it is pulled tight to eliminate wrinkles.

2. Sand and finish the side bumpers; place them appropriately around the board on top of the felt covering.

3. Screw in ¾″ screws from underneath the board. They should go through the board, through the felt, and into the bumpers to hold them in place.

4. Mark on the felt the pattern of lines, dots, and shooter designations (use a felt-tipped marker).

(This shooting surface may be constructed using other materials, such as indoor-outdoor carpet and masking tape.)

MARBLES PRE-ESTABLISHED-RULES SHEET

The following rules will remain in force throughout the activity. They are *nonnegotiable,* and they are implemented by the treasurer.

General

1. There will be six rounds.

2. In each round there will be four phases: bargaining, preparing the shooting surface, shooting, and payoff.

3. The treasurer determines the placement of marbles and towers and distributes payoffs.

4. Dowels are distributed arbitrarily before round 1. At the end of each subsequent round, dowels are distributed as follows: the shooter with the most marbles gets the longest dowel, the shooter with the second highest number of marbles receives the next-longest dowel, and so on. If there is a tie, the distribution is alphabetical within the tie, i.e, shooter B before shooter C.

5. Additional rules may be made by the rule maker. A new rule is enforceable after it has been posted for all to see.

Bargaining

6. No bargaining phase may exceed three minutes.

7. A "valid agreement," which determines the distribution of bonus marbles, can exist between at least two shooters whose dowel tower is higher than any other.

8. In the event that no valid agreement is reached within the three minutes of bargaining, no bonus marbles are allocated for that round.

Preparing the Shooting Surface

9. Only the treasurer may place materials on or remove materials from the shooting surface.

10. The treasurer may "sell" public-job marbles to the rule maker and protection marbles to the rule enforcer. The buyers indicate to him where these marbles are to be placed.

Structured Experience 165

11. All marbles on the shooting surface revert to the treasurer and are removed from the shooting surface at the end of each round.

Shooting

12. Each shooter is permitted one shot per round.

13. Shots must be taken from the shooter's designated shooting area, from behind the line marked on the shooting surface.

14. In each round, the shooter having the least number of marbles shoots first, the shooter with the second-least number shoots second, and so on, with the shooter having the most marbles taking his turn last. Ties are resolved alphabetically, e.g., in round 1 the sequence is A, B, C, D, E.

15. Shooting stops immediately in any round during which the tower is toppled. (Disregard accidental bumps of the playing surface.) If this occurs, remaining shooters lose their turns for that round.

Payoff

16. The following schedule determines the payoff for particular events:

Occurrence	Payoff (in marbles)
Hitting job marble(s)	+3 per
Hitting public-job marble(s)	+3 per
Dislodging trouble marble(s)	−1 per Lego block underneath
Encroaching on shooting surface	−2
Tower remaining intact throughout round	Distribution of announced bonus

17. Disputes are decided by the judge, who is not permitted to observe the activity on the shooting surface.

18. The winner is the individual (other than the treasurer or the observer) who has accumulated the most marbles after the sixth-round payoff.

MARBLES ROLE-DESCRIPTIONS SHEET

Shooter

The following are special instructions for your role. *Do not reveal this information to anyone.*

Your objective is to win, i.e., to end round six with the most marbles. You may make *any* deals or agreements that you think will help you accomplish this objective. These arrangements may be initiated with other shooters, the rule maker, the rule enforcer, or the judge.

During the bargaining phase, you may enter into an agreement with one or more of the other shooters for the bonus marbles. This agreement is symbolized by stacking the dowel pieces of the persons in the agreement end on end to form a tower. In order for you to be eligible to win bonus marbles, your dowel piece must be a part of the highest tower.

If you are not a party to the "valid agreement," you may attempt to shoot down the tower during your turn.

Rule Maker

The following are special instructions for your role.

Your objective is to make things run as smoothly as possible and, by doing so, to prove that you are the right person for the job. You may make any rules or agreements that you think will help this to happen. Agreements may be initiated with shooters, the rule enforcer, or the judge.

You are empowered to impose your rules in addition to the pre-established, non-negotiable ones. In order for your rules to be enforceable, they must be posted where all players can see them. Some ideas are: tax levies, salaries for nonshooters, penalties, supplemental bonuses, and distribution of income from your rules.

During the preparing-the-shooting-surface phase of each round, you may purchase public-job marbles for two marbles each and indicate to the treasurer where you want them to be placed on the board.

Rule Enforcer

The following are special instructions for your role.

Your objective is to be fair and to prove yourself worthy of re-election. You may make *any* deals or agreements that you think will help you to accomplish this objective. This bargaining may be initiated with shooters, the rule maker, or the judge.

Your responsibility is to report to the treasurer any infractions of pre-established rules, and to *enforce* those rules posted by the rule maker.

During the preparing-the-shooting-surface phase of each round, you may purchase protection marbles for two marbles each and indicate to the treasurer where you want them to be placed on the board.

Judge

The following are special instructions for your role.

Your objective is to be fair and to prove yourself worthy of re-election. You may make *any* deals or agreements that you think will help you to accomplish this objective. This bargaining may be initiated with shooters, the rule maker, or the rule enforcer.

Your responsibility is to make binding decisions when disputes are brought to you. You may impose penalties at your discretion. You may *not* observe the activity on the shooting surface.

Treasurer

The following are special instructions for your role.

Your objective is to ensure an orderly succession of rounds. Your responsibilities include the following: implementing the rules, enforcing the pre-established rules, preparing the playing surface, and collecting and disbursing marbles appropriately. You are not eligible to win.

Preliminary to Round 1

1. Give a cup containing five marbles to each of the following participants: the five shooters, the rule maker, the rule enforcer, and the judge.

2. Arbitrarily distribute the five dowels among the shooters, one to each.

Rounds 1 to 6 (Repeat the following four phases in each round.)

1. Bargaining
   a. Distribute the dowels.
   b. Announce the number of bonus marbles available for each round (in this order: 5, 10, 15, 20, 25, 30).
   c. Start the timer.

d. Determine whether a valid agreement has been reached and announce which shooter(s) may receive the potential bonus.

e. If no valid agreement has been reached in the time permitted, announce the termination of the bargaining phase.

2. Preparing the Shooting Surface

a. Distribute the appropriate number of job marbles (green) randomly on the dots.

b. Place the trouble marbles (gold) in position on their appropriately sized Lego supports.

c. Place the valid-agreement tower (if there is one) in the center.

d. Offer public-job marbles (blue) for sale to the rule maker; if a purchase is made, place the sold marble(s) where the purchaser indicates. Follow the same procedure for selling protection marbles (large) to the rule enforcer.

Round	Number of Bonus Marbles	Number of Job Marbles	Number of Lego Blocks for Trouble-Marble Supports
1	5	6	1
2	10	3	2
3	15	4	3
4	20	6	4
5	25	3	5
6	30	5	6

3. Shooting

a. Determine the order of shooting.

b. Announce the beginning of the shooting phase.

4. Payoff

a. The appropriate transaction is carried out after each shooter completes his turn.

b. If a valid-agreement tower has remained intact throughout the shooting phase, disburse the appropriate number of bonus marbles.

Observer

Your task is to watch the activity to make a *brief* report after rounds 2, 4, and 6.

You are not eligible to win.

You cannot be a party to any deal.

Some things to observe are: influence, feelings, communication patterns, and reactions to rules.

Structured Experience 165

166. AGENDA SETTING: A TEAM-BUILDING STARTER

Goals

I. To create and rank-order an agenda for a team-building session.

II. To generate ownership of and commitment to commonly perceived problems facing a work group.

III. To develop effective listening skills.

Group Size

Varies. (This structured experience is intended as an initial activity in a team-development program. The "team" may be any work unit, such as a committee, task force, production line, or decision-making group.)

Time Required

Approximately one hour.

Materials

I. Newsprint, felt-tipped markers, and masking tape.

II. Paper and a pencil for each participant.

Physical Setting

A room large enough for pairs of participants to meet privately. Wall space is needed for posting.

Process

I. The facilitator discusses the goals of the activity and gives a brief overview of the design.

II. Team members are instructed to pair off by selecting a person with whom they have not talked recently.

III. When pairs are assembled in separate places in the room, the facilitator tells them to take turns interviewing each other. The topic for the interview is "What problem situations should we work on in this team-building session?" Each participant will have five minutes to interview his partner. Interviewers are *not* to take notes, but they are to be prepared to report what their interviewee said.

IV. After the interviewing phase is completed, the team is reassembled in a circle. (The facilitator remains outside the circle.) Each member takes a turn reporting to the team (not to the facilitator) what his partner said. The facilitator lists on newsprint each member's suggested problem situations (in the member's own words). Each interviewee then "corrects the record" by adding anything that the interviewer left out or by adjusting any misperceptions. During this phase, team members may respond only by asking questions for clarification.

V. The lists of problem situations are posted on a wall, and the items are numbered. Duplicates are combined or are given the same number.

VI. The facilitator instructs each team member to select, by *number,* the three problem situations that he believes are most important. Then the facilitator tallies on the newsprint the number of members who have indicated each of the items.

VII. The facilitator posts a new list of the items with the highest frequencies in the tally.

VIII. Each participant is instructed to *rank-order* these problem situations independently, in terms of which are most important. The rank "1" is to be assigned to the item that the member believes *must* be discussed if the team-building session is to be successful. The second most pressing situation is ranked "2," and so on.

IX. The facilitator tallies the ranks assigned to each of the items by asking how many members ranked item A as 1, 2, 3, etc. (If there are more than six or seven items, the tally can be based on a "high, medium, or low" ranking.)

X. The facilitator posts the final agenda on newsprint. He leads a discussion of reactions to the agenda-setting process.

Variations

I. The interview time can be varied to take into account the length of the team-building session. In a brief meeting, the interviewers can ask for the *one* problem situation that needs to be faced by the team.

II. The leader of the team (instead of the facilitator) can function as the recorder.

Similar Structured Experiences: *Vol. II:* Structured Experience **45;** *Vol. III:* **66;** *'73 Annual:* **87.**

Suggested Instruments: *'75 Annual:* "Problem-Analysis Questionnaire," "Diagnosing Organization Ideology."

Lecturette Sources: *'72 Annual:* "Openness, Collusion and Feedback"; *'73 Annual:* "The Sensing Interview"; *'74 Annual:* "Team-Building."

Submitted by John E. Jones.

Structured Experience 166

Notes on the Use of "Agenda Setting":

167. CUPS: A POWER EXPERIENCE

Goals

I. To increase awareness of the meanings of power.

II. To experience giving, receiving, and not receiving power.

Group Size

Eight to twelve participants.

Time Required

Approximately two hours.

Materials

I. Two paper or styrofoam cups for each participant.

II. Paper and a pencil for each participant.

III. Felt-tipped markers.

Physical Setting

The group is seated in a circle.

Process

I. The facilitator briefly introduces the activity. He distributes two cups, paper, and a pencil to each participant. Felt-tipped markers are passed around, and each participant writes his name on his cups and places them on the floor in front of him.

II. The group is led through a brief fantasy in which each participant imagines a situation in which he would be very powerful in the group. The participants are directed to imagine letting their power flow from themselves into their cups.

III. Participants are asked to define their concept of power, to write these thoughts on two slips of paper, and to place a slip in each of their cups.

IV. The facilitator directs participants to spend a moment selecting two persons in the group to whom they would give their power. Participants are instructed to take out the slips, write one person's name on each slip, and place it back inside the cup.

V. Participants are told that they will be giving away their cups. Before doing so, each participant privately predicts how many cups he will receive. The facilitator announces that each participant is to state the basis for his decision to the persons receiving his cups. Then, one at a time, participants give away their cups to the persons of their choice.

VI. The facilitator instructs participants to write down their personal reactions and to share these with a partner.

VII. A series of group-on-group discussions is held to process reactions. The first "inside" group is composed of persons receiving no cups, the second "inside" group is composed of those receiving one or two cups, and the third "inside" group includes persons receiving three or more cups.

VIII. The facilitator leads the total group in a discussion of the meaning of power.

IX. The facilitator announces that participants receiving cups will have an opportunity to use their newly acquired power. One minute for each cup received will be allocated for using the power.

X. Recipients of power cups are given a few moments to think about how they will use their power with each person who gave it to them. Those receiving no cups are to predict how the persons to whom they gave power will use it.

XI. While the total group observes, each recipient of power carries out his plan with the persons who gave him cups. After each power enactment, the group offers feedback.

XII. The facilitator leads a discussion of the entire activity, focusing on its goals.

Variations

I. The structured experience can be either interrupted or stopped at the end of step VIII.

II. Traits other than power (trust, dependency, etc.) can be used.

III. The group can agree on a definition of power before members decide to whom they will give their cups.

IV. Instead of the process described in steps IX, X, and XI, the power can be "inverted." That is, the cups can be redistributed to those receiving few or none. These persons then plan how they will use their power, either collectively or separately.

Similar Structured Experiences: *Vol. III:* Structured Experiences **58, 59;** *'73 Annual:* **98;** *Vol. IV:* **124;** *'74 Annual:* **146.**

Suggested Instrument: *'75 Annual:* "Diagnosing Organization Ideology."

Notes on the Use of "Cups":

Submitted by Anthony J. Reilly.

Structured Experience 167

168. ADJECTIVES: FEEDBACK

Goals

I. To help participants clarify values that apply to human relationships.

II. To establish the norms of soliciting and giving both positive and negative feedback.

Group Size

Unlimited.

Time Required

Approximately one hour.

Materials

I. Newsprint, felt-tipped markers, and masking tape.

II. Paper and a pencil for each participant.

Physical Setting

A room with wall space for posting adjective lists so that everyone can see them.

Process

I. Without discussing the goals of the activity, the facilitator announces that participants are about to take a two-item "test." He gives the following directions: "Item 1. Think of the *one* person in the world (other than yourself) with whom you have the *most* satisfactory relationship. Write three adjectives that describe that person." (A two-to-three-minute pause.) "By now you can imagine what item 2 is. Think of the *one* person in the world with whom you have the *least* satisfactory relationship. This should be a different person. Now write three adjectives that describe *that* person." (A two-to-three-minute pause.)

II. The facilitator explains that the test gives a rough indication of one's values; that is, the adjectives say more about the writer than about the persons described. On the basis of the adjectives they listed, participants are instructed to write a sentence that begins with the phrase "I am the kind of person who values . . ."

III. Participants form pairs with nearby persons. They share what the test indicated about them, but they do *not* discuss the persons about whom they wrote the adjectives. (Five minutes.)

IV. The facilitator asks participants to contribute the adjectives they have written under item 1; he lists these on newsprint in rough alphabetical order. Then the adjectives from item 2 are listed on newsprint. These two lists are displayed side by side on a wall so that all participants can easily read them.

V. The facilitator announces that the next phase of the activity will involve feedback. He instructs participants to select someone with whom to share both positive and negative feedback. The facilitator indicates that one member of each pair is to *solicit* feedback about himself from both the negative and positive lists *before* he describes himself. Then the other partner does the same. (Twenty minutes.)

VI. The facilitator leads a discussion of the entire experience. He may wish to solicit comments about the tendency to offer evaluative feedback to others and about the feelings associated with giving and receiving both positive and negative feedback.

Variations

I. The number of adjectives in each of the two items can be varied; e.g., for large groups, only one adjective may be requested.

II. The adjective subject can be varied. Other topics might be job situations, discipline, best/worse boss (colleague, employee, etc.).

III. A meal break can follow step IV in order for the lists to be duplicated and distributed to all participants.

IV. Instead of feedback (or in addition to it), the lists can be used for self-assessment and self-disclosure.

Similar Structured Experiences: *Vol. III:* Structured Experience **58;** *Vol. IV:* **112.**
Suggested Instruments: *'72 Annual:* "Supervisory Attitudes: The X-Y Scale"; *'73 Annual:* "Scale of Feelings and Behavior of Love," "The Involvement Inventory"; *'74 Annual:* "Self-Disclosure Questionnaire."
Lecturette Sources: *'72 Annual:* "Openness, Collusion and Feedback"; *'75 Annual:* "Giving Feedback: An Interpersonal Skill."

Notes on the Use of "Adjectives":

Submitted by John E. Jones.

169. DYADIC RENEWAL: A PROGRAM FOR DEVELOPING ONGOING RELATIONSHIPS

Goal

To periodically explore various aspects of a relationship through mutual self-disclosure and risk taking.

Group Size

Any number of pairs of participants who are interested in enriching their relationships.

Time Required

A minimum of two hours. (May be scheduled in several sessions.)

Materials

One Dyadic Renewal Booklet for each participant. The booklet should be prepared in such a way that participants are presented statements one at a time. (Preassembled, reusable booklets may be ordered from University Associates. The price is one dollar each, and the minimum order is twelve copies.)

Physical Setting

A room large enough for the dyads to meet privately.

Process

I. The facilitator discusses how relationships are enhanced by periodic self-disclosure and feedback.

II. Participants pair up with another person with whom they have some history of interaction on a personal level. Each pair sits together, away from other pairs.

III. Two copies of the Dyadic Renewal Booklet are given to each pair. The total group is told how much time is allotted for the activity.

IV. Following the activity, the total group reassembles. The facilitator assists in processing the event by encouraging each participant to share what he learned about himself from the experience. (It is important to remember that an expectation of confidentiality is established by the directions.)

Variations

I. Groups of various sizes (triads, quartets, etc.) can utilize the Dyadic Renewal Booklet. (This variation tends to take more time.)

II. When the laboratory design includes the development of a continuing personal relationship with another person, "Dyadic Renewal" can be used in conjunction with "Dyadic Encounter" (*Vol. I:* Structured Experience 21).

III. Items can be posted on newsprint to stimulate group discussion. Subgroups of people who have an interpersonal relationship with each other can be formed to exchange responses to selected items.

Similar Structured Experiences: *Vol. I:* Structured Experience **21**; *Vol. II:* **25, 45**; *Vol. III:* **70**; *Vol. IV:* **116, 118**.

Suggested Instruments: *'72 Annual:* "Interpersonal Relationship Rating Scale"; *'73 Annual:* "Scale of Feelings and Behavior of Love," "The Involvement Inventory"; *'74 Annual:* "Interpersonal Communication Inventory," "Self-Disclosure Questionnaire"; *'75 Annual:* "Scale of Marriage Problems."

Lecturette Sources: *'72 Annual:* "Openness, Collusion and Feedback"; *'73 Annual:* "The Johari Window: A Model for Soliciting and Giving Feedback"; *'75 Annual:* "Giving Feedback: An Interpersonal Skill."

Notes on the Use of "Dyadic Renewal":

Submitted by Colleen A. Kelley and J. Stephen Colladay.

DYADIC RENEWAL BOOKLET

The facilitator should prepare a booklet for each participant, with the pages numbered as follows:

1

DYADIC RENEWAL: A PROGRAM FOR DEVELOPING
ONGOING RELATIONSHIPS

2

Read silently. Do not look ahead or thumb through this booklet.

Dyadic Renewal is a series of open-ended statements intended to help you examine your relationship with another person and practice new modes of interacting. This discussion is intended to be confidential.

One of the underlying assumptions of this booklet is that all relationships periodically need renewal. This program provides an easy and nonthreatening structure to help you take time out from everyday living to look at yourselves, at who you are, and at where you are going.

3

One important element in relationships is good communication. In order to facilitate this, listening checks have been placed at appropriate intervals. A listening check involves repeating your partner's statement in your own words, in order to assure that you have heard it correctly.

Opportunities have also been provided for you to talk about your feelings and to express yourself nonverbally as you go through the booklet.

It is important that you:

1. Be open and accepting of your partner's responses.
2. Talk about your own feelings. Use "I" statements rather than "you" statements.
3. Feel free to skip any item.
4. Use this activity to share information, rather than to solve problems.
5. Be willing to take risks.

4

Again, it is important that you do not look ahead since the program is based on the assumption that spontaneous, here-and-now answers are best. Thinking ahead for an answer will block your hearing of your partner's response.

Directions

Both persons are to complete each statement. You are encouraged to amplify the discussion by adding to the statement. One person should respond initially to items on even-numbered pages. The other person responds initially to items on odd-numbered pages. (Do not write in the booklet.)

If your partner has finished reading, go on to the next page and begin.

5

The first time we met was . . .

6

The amount of time we have known each other is . . .

7

The kind of relationship we have is . . .

8

One adjective to describe our relationship would be . . .

9

One way in which we are alike is . . .

Structured Experience 169

10

One way in which we are different is . . .

11

If our relationship were a film, it would be called . . .

12

A peak experience in our relationship was . . .

13

A place I would like to share with you is . . .

14

I find your friends to be . . .

15

When we meet new people, I . . .

16

When I am with you in a social situation, I feel . . .

17

One of the most "fun" things we ever did was . . .

18

The needs you satisfy in me are . . .

19

Some of my needs that are not being completely satisfied are . . .

20

Right now I feel . . .

21

A song that reminds me of you is . . .

22

The amount of time I spend alone is . . .

Listening check: "Are you saying that . . . ?"

23

One of your greatest assets is . . .

24

I am proud of you when . . .

Structured Experience 169

25

Something you have helped me to learn about myself is . . .

26

One of the feelings with which I have the most trouble is . . .

27

The way I deal with troublesome feelings now is . . .

Listening check: "What I hear you saying is . . ."

28

I feel indecisive when . . .

29

I am most "suspicious" of you when . . .

30

I assume you know that . . .

31

If I could make you over, I would never change . . .

32

You are most helpful when . . .

Express to your partner how you are feeling right now without using words.

33

I am afraid . . .

34

I like it when you . . .

35

You annoy me when you . . .

36

One thing I regret having done is . . .

37

A habit of mine that bothers me most is . . .

38

Your greatest strength is . . .

39

I do not like it when you . . .

40

Something I dislike about you that we seldom talk about is . . .

Structured Experience 169

41

I have the most fun with you when . . .

42

If I had all the money in the world, I would . . .

43

A frequent fantasy I have about you is . . .

44

When we have an intellectual discussion . . .

45

You tend to talk a lot about . . .

46

When I don't want to answer questions, I . . .

47

When I can't express something to you, I . . .

48

This experience . . .

(This is a convenient place to interrupt the activity.)

49

A thing that is helping us to grow closer is . . .

50

The things I most like to do with you are . . .

51

I tend not to tell you about . . .

52

Something I am usually reluctant to discuss is . . .

53

Something I have always wondered about is . . .

54

I think you avoid me when . . .

55

An area in which I would like to feel more equal to you is . . .

56

I feel inferior to you when . . .

Structured Experience 169

57

I feel rebellious when . . .

Try to make your partner laugh without using words.

58

I need you most when . . .

59

To keep from being hurt, I . . .

60

It hurts me when . . .

61

When I hurt you, I . . .

62

I get discouraged or frustrated when . . .

63

I think you are unfair when you . . .

64

When you are pouting, I feel . . .

Listening check: "It sounds to me as if you are saying that . . ."

65

The things that hold us together are . . .

66

The habit you have that bothers me most is . . .

67

I become most defensive when you . . .

68

I was most angry with you when . . .

69

When we fight . . .

70

When I feel as if I have lost, I . . .

71

Right now I am feeling . . .

72

I think that you do not give me a chance to . . .

Structured Experience 169

73

An important thing or issue between us right now is . . .

Listening check: "What I think you are saying is . . ."

74

I find that being open with you is . . .

75

One thing I have always wanted to talk more about is . . .

76

I wish you would let me know when I . . .

77

I think it would be fun to . . .

78

If I wanted to make you laugh, I would . . .

79

A pattern I see in our relationship is . . .

Try to tell your partner how you are feeling without using words.

80

The part of my body that I like most is . . .

81

The part of my body that I like least is . . .

82

What I like most about your body is . . .

83

The ways I like you to touch me are . . .

84

Right now I am feeling . . .

85

My attitudes about premarital and extramarital sex are . . .

86

I feel jealous when . . .

87

I feel most tender toward you when . . .

Listening check: "I think I hear you saying that . . ."

Structured Experience 169

88

One of the times that bothered me most in our relationship was . . .

89

What I like best about our relationship is . . .

90

In the future, I would like our relationship to become more . . .

91

The type of relationship I do not want to develop with you is . . .

92

The thing I value most in life is . . .

93

I believe in and am committed to . . .

94

In five years, I see us . . .

95

You may wish to continue this discussion by generating a list of topics of your own choosing and responding to those that interest you most, e.g., careers, money, family, sex.

You may also wish to set a date to use Dyadic Renewal again with your partner. Relationships periodically *need* renewal.

----

170. PERSON PERCEPTION: FEEDBACK

Goals

I. To provide feedback to individual group members about how they are perceived by others.

II. To help participants clarify what underlies their tendency to categorize other persons.

Group Size

No more than twelve participants.

Time Required

Approximately one hour.

Materials

I. A copy of the Person Perception Inventory Sheet and of the Person Perception Recording Sheet for each participant.

II. A pencil for each participant.

Physical Setting

Participants should be seated comfortably for writing.

Process

I. The facilitator discusses the goals and gives a brief overview of the activity.

II. He distributes a copy of the Person Perception Inventory Sheet and a pencil to each participant. He reads the directions aloud and answers any questions. Participants are instructed to complete the inventory.

III. The facilitator hands out copies of the Person Perception Recording Sheet and explains its use.

IV. The facilitator calls for a volunteer to share his data. Other members record information relevant to themselves. Then other participants volunteer in turn. (During this phase only questions for clarification are allowed—no reactions.)

V. After all the perceptions have been published, the facilitator instructs participants to study their perceptions of others to determine what personal dimensions they use in sorting out people. The group discusses these generalizations.

VI. The facilitator focuses on members one at a time to determine their reactions to the feedback they have received, and calls for group discussion after each member's response.

VII. The facilitator leads a discussion of the entire experience, focusing on such topics as labeling, projection, characterization, and validation by consensus.

Variations

I. The subgroupings can be posted on newsprint.

II. A tally can be made of how many times each group member is paired with each other member, using a form such as the following:

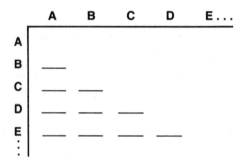

III. Some of the subgroups can be convened for the purpose of determining what they believe they have in common.

IV. Group characteristics can be predetermined by the facilitator.

V. Group members who are least frequently perceived as similar on the Person Perception Inventory Sheet can be paired and instructed to talk about both their differences and their similarities. (The same procedure can be used with pairs of persons most frequently perceived as similar on the Person Perception Inventory Sheet.)

Similar Structured Experiences: *Vol. II:* Structured Experiences **42, 43** (numbers 6, 7, 8, 11); *Vol III:* **57, 58;** *Vol. IV:* **107;** *'74 Annual:* **129.**

Suggested Instruments: *'72 Annual:* "Interpersonal Relationship Rating Scale"; *'73 Annual:* "Scale of Feelings and Behavior of Love," "The Involvement Inventory"; *'74 Annual:* "Self-Disclosure Questionnaire."

Lecturette Sources: *'72 Annual:* "Openness, Collusion and Feedback"; *'75 Annual:* "Giving Feedback: An Interpersonal Skill."

Reference

Kelly, G. A. *Theory of personality: The psychology of personal constructs.* New York: W. W. Norton, 1963.

Notes on the Use of "Person Perception":

Based on materials submitted by Robert H. Dolliver.

Structured Experience 170

PERSON PERCEPTION INVENTORY SHEET

Instructions: In the spaces below, you are to form two subgroups from the membership of your group (including yourself). Record those characteristics that describe the ways in which the members of each subgroup are alike. Persons who do not fit into your two-category system are to be listed as "remaining members," along with their unique characteristic(s).

Subgroup I

Members:

Common characteristic(s):

Subgroup II

Members:

Common characteristic(s):

Remaining Members

Name   Unique Characteristic(s):

PERSON PERCEPTION RECORDING SHEET

Instructions: On this sheet, record the perceptions which other group members have of
you. Write the name of the person giving you feedback, the names of the other
members with whom you were categorized, and the characteristic(s) of that group.
If you were not grouped, record the unique characteristic(s) attributed to you.

Member Giving Feedback	Subgroup Members	Subgroup Characteristic(s)
_____	_____	_____
_____	_____	_____
_____	_____	_____
_____	_____	_____
_____	_____	_____
_____	_____	_____
_____	_____	_____
_____	_____	_____
_____	_____	_____
_____	_____	_____

Structured Experience 170

171. ROLE CLARIFICATION: A TEAM-BUILDING ACTIVITY

Goals

I. To clarify both expectations that team members have of others' roles and conceptions that team members have of their own roles.

II. To promote renegotiation of role responsibilities within a work unit.

III. To teach a process of role adjustment that can become a work-group norm.

Group Size

No more than twelve members.

Time Required

A minimum of three hours.

Materials

I. Newsprint, felt-tipped markers, and masking tape.

II. Paper and a pencil for each participant.

Physical Setting

A private room with wall space for posting.

Process

I. The facilitator presents a lecturette on the four aspects of role:*
1. *Role expectations*—what others think the person is responsible for and how he should do it;
2. *Role conception*—what the person thinks his job is and how he has been "taught" to do it;
3. *Role acceptance*—what the person is willing to do;
4. *Role behavior*—what the person actually does.

The facilitator briefly discusses the goals of the activity. He indicates that members will be asked to write several sets of notes and that they will be expected to talk about what they write.

II. The facilitator instructs team members to make notes about their own jobs in terms of the four aspects of role discussed. (Twenty minutes.)

---

*See G. W. Allport, *Pattern and Growth in Personality*, New York: Holt, Rinehart and Winston, 1961.

III. The facilitator calls for a volunteer who wants to clarify his role within the work group. While the other group members make notes on their understanding of this volunteer's responsibilities, the facilitator briefs the volunteer on the sequence of activities that will follow. (Ten minutes.)

IV. The volunteer states what he thinks the other members' "role expectations" of his role are, and the facilitator lists the key points on newsprint. (Only questions of clarification are allowed from other team members.)

V. The volunteer then questions the other team members and lists on newsprint their actual expectations. (The facilitator intervenes only to keep the volunteer listening accurately and nondefensively.)

VI. The facilitator leads a discussion of the confirmed and misperceived expectations.

VII. The volunteer discusses his own "role conception," while the facilitator makes notes on newsprint. (Only questions of clarification are accepted.)

VIII. The facilitator conducts a renegotiation session in which the volunteer makes a new contract with the other team members.

IX. Steps III through VIII are repeated with other volunteers.

X. The facilitator leads a discussion of the role-clarification process. He emphasizes the need to renegotiate expectations periodically.

Variations

I. Step II can be assigned as prework for the session.

II. To clarify his role, a volunteer can choose a subgroup of those persons with whom he is most interdependent.

III. The entire process can be used as a third-party intervention, e.g., in a supervisor-subordinate relationship.

Similar Structured Experiences: *Vol. II:* Structured Experience **38**; *Vol. III:* **67, 68.**
Suggested Instruments: *'73 Annual:* "LEAD (Leadership: Employee-Orientation and Differentiation) Questionnaire"; *'75 Annual:* "Problem-Analysis Questionnaire," "Decision-Style Inventory," "Diagnosing Organization Ideology."
Lecturette Sources: *'72 Annual:* "Notes on Freedom"; *'73 Annual:* "Planned Renegotiation: A Norm-Setting OD Intervention"; *'74 Annual:* "Team-Building."

Submitted by John E. Jones.

Structured Experience 171

Notes on the Use of "Role Clarification":

172. GROUP COMPOSITION: A SELECTION ACTIVITY

Goals

I. To explore the process of selection of group members.

II. To assist facilitators in identifying their biases about group composition.

III. To study similarities and differences between personal growth and psychotherapy groups.

Group Size

An unlimited number of groups of three to six members each.

Time Required

Approximately one and one-half hours.

Materials

I. A copy of the Group Composition Candidate Profile Sheet for each participant.

II. Newsprint, masking tape, and a felt-tipped marker.

III. Paper and a pencil for each participant.

Process

I. Without discussing the goals of the activity, the facilitator distributes copies of the Group Composition Candidate Profile Sheet and instructs participants to study it silently. (Ten minutes.)

II. He forms subgroups of three to six members each. The subgroups are seated separately and instructed that each is to select a group of no more than eight persons from among the candidates on the list. The selection is to be a consensus decision. (Twenty minutes.)

III. As soon as the groups have begun the task, the facilitator *privately* tells half of the subgroups to select candidates for a psychotherapy group. He tells the other half of the subgroups (*privately*) to select candidates for a personal growth group.

IV. After the selection task, the subgroups are directed to abstract the principles, values, and biases that prompted their choices. (Ten minutes.)

V. The selections from each subgroup are posted on newsprint. The facilitator then leads a general discussion. He may deliver a lecturette on group composition and the distinctions between growth groups and psychotherapy groups.*

Variations

I. The list of candidates can be given to members of an ongoing psychotherapy or personal growth group with instructions that they choose two or three candidates as new members of their own group. The group can be directed to reach agreement through balloting, power plays, or consensus seeking. Processing can be done in terms of group biases, values, norm development, or inclusion issues.

II. After a group has been composed from the profile sheet, members can be assigned to role play specific candidates. The role play can be used as an exercise in intervention practice or as a dramatization of critical incidents.

III. Co-facilitators can fantasize critical incidents that might happen both in and out of the meetings of the group that they have composed. They then share these expectations with each other and indicate whether they would promote or discourage such occurrences.

Similar Structured Experiences: *Vol. I:* Structured Experience **24**; *Vol. IV:* **113, 124**; *'74 Annual:* **135**; *'75 Annual:* **148.**

Suggested Instruments: *'72 Annual:* "Intervention Style Survey," "Non-Research Uses of the Group Leadership Questionnaire (GTQ-C)"; *'73 Annual:* "Helping Relationship Inventory"; *'74 Annual:* "Reactions to Group Situations Test."

Lecturette Sources: *'72 Annual:* "Types of Growth Groups"; *'74 Annual:* "Therapeutic Intervention and the Perception of Process"; *'75 Annual:* "Therapy or Personal Growth?", "Co-Facilitating."

---

*On the Group Composition Candidate Profile Sheet, those members whose names form the acronym SICK (Stan, Ivan, Charleen, Karen) have profiles slanted toward psychopathology; those profiles forming the acronym WELL (Will, Ellen, Len, Lois) are slanted toward health; while those that spell NORM (Nancy, Olima, Roger, Murray) are purposely ambiguous.

Based on material submitted by Gerald M. Phillips. Revised by Anthony G. Banet, Jr.

Notes on the Use of "Group Composition":

GROUP COMPOSITION CANDIDATE PROFILE SHEET

CHARLEEN. White, female, age 29; B.A. (philosophy); employed as newsletter editor in a manufacturing company; reports no hobbies or activities.

"*I like the changes in the Catholic Church. I only wish I could take part in what is happening, but I seem to be mostly a spectator, not a participant. I tend to be liberal in politics but I'm really apathetic when it comes to action.*

"*I don't understand my own sex drives. A few years ago I had both lesbian and straight experiences. Now I don't have experiences at all, not even temptations. I have often wanted to try drugs, pot especially, but I don't seem to be able to muster the courage. My highly moral superego tells me it is not worth it.*

"*There is nothing distinguishing about me. I read a lot, spend a lot of time just thinking—alone. I wish I could teach in a junior college somewhere. I wanted to, but I felt I wouldn't be any good in the classroom.*"

Physical description: Charleen is tall and thin. She has short red hair. She dresses neatly but in very bright colors and clashing combinations.

Personal concern: Charleen complains that she cannot talk well with others. She reports that her mind wanders and that she cannot concentrate. She complains of loneliness and boredom and has no motivation to take an active part in anything. She was hospitalized briefly five years ago due to depression and a halfhearted suicide attempt.

KAREN. White, female, age 23; works part time as a clerk in an adult bookstore near a college campus; takes classes occasionally.

"*So I was born a Jew, but I could care less. My parents think I'm dirt, but I think they are part of the establishment that is wrecking this country, so we don't see each other much. They are all for me as long as I am a good, husband-hunting little cutie, but when I want to go my own way, they jump all over me.*

"*I dig sex a lot. I make it with my man and with lots of other guys too. So what? I've been using drugs for quite a while. Maybe if we all tripped together we could get the establishment going right. I really don't know what to do with my life. I may not live to be thirty-five.*"

Physical description: Karen is "ordinary" looking. She dresses with studied slovenliness. She is a bit heavy and big-busted; her hair is relatively unkempt. She rarely smiles. She typically wears tight jeans and loose tops.

Personal concern: Karen feels that other females resent her. She has no female friends. She reports that she sleeps with her boss and the other clerks, as well as with the man she is living with and his friends. Karen says she wants someone to help her become more persuasive because she feels a "call" to sell the world on tripping to find "perfect peace."

ROGER. White, male, age 33; engineer; unmarried; reports memberships in religious and conservative political organizations.

"I want to work for a large corporation and help participate in the building of our American economy. I want to be a good person and to be married. I think men and women should be virgins when they marry because that is what God wants. If people in our country would only become more religious, we could end poverty and drug use and bad movies and other things. I work as hard as I can so I can be a true witness of Christ."

Physical description: Roger is about 6 feet tall, slim, with pale brown hair and blue eyes. He has some acne scars. He wears glasses, carries a calculator at his belt, and wears his hair closely cropped.

Personal concern: Roger reports that he does not have many friends. He spends much of his recreation time alone, at films, lectures, and concerts. He reports that people in his apartment complex do not like to talk to him. He talks a lot about his religion and what it means to him. He thinks that the people who are avoiding him are doing so because they are uninterested in religion. He says that he grew up as an only child, and he wonders a lot about his impact on other people. He is concerned that he may be past the "marrying age."

OLIMA X. Black, female, age 29; operator of a black "self-help" machine-repair shop; claims Muslim religion; one year of college.

"I dropped out of college because it was a white man's scene. There is no place for a woman and no place for blacks. I became a Muslim because there is nothing in Christianity for black people. It's time we got our own religion going. Jesus was a black man, and that is why the Jews killed him. I want to help my people be themselves.

"I'm not talking to you about sex or drugs. You whites think all we blacks want is sex and drugs. You want to be an anthropologist, you turn black and live with us, and then you'll know how we live."

Physical description: Olima is short, stout, and very dark and wears a high Afro hairdo and Afro-style clothing. She wears a medallion around her neck and fingers it constantly.

Personal concern: Olima makes it clear that she trusts only blacks. She demands a black group leader and says that she will not work with anyone else. She reports that she feels she needs to learn how to control her hostilities so she can be more effective in "bringing the revolution." Olima says she knows she turns some people off, but that she is willing to sacrifice close relationships if that is what it takes to produce social change. She reports some insomnia and worry over her worth as a person.

Structured Experience 172

STAN. White, male, age 24; plays on the taxi squad for a professional football team and works as a part-time bartender; no religion.

"*As far as politics go, I think we need somebody in our country to stop the march of communism.*

"*I dig sex. Sex is what women think about when I'm around. I never stayed with a woman after she didn't satisfy me any more. There isn't a woman I couldn't satisfy. Don't ask me about homosexual stuff—those dudes really bug me.*

"*I'm going to make the team one of these days. If I don't make it this season, maybe I'll jump to Canada. I never finished my degree at Southern. I must have gone to seven different schools—those egghead types don't know about real life. So I'll need to make money playing pro ball to open a bar.*"

Physical description: Stan is 6 feet, 4 inches tall, weighs 244 pounds. He looks like the lineman that he is.

Personal concern: Stan expresses uneasiness about the way people respond to him. He thinks he is losing his friends. He is bothered about his legal difficulties—six arrests in the past two years for the "minor" offenses of passing bad checks and possession of marijuana. He is not interested in his relationships with women because he sees them only as sexual objects, but he is concerned that his male friends regard him as "an animal" and are not aware of how sensitive he really is. He was in counseling several years ago, but says, "It didn't work out. I'm smarter than most of those guys."

MURRAY. White, male, age 26; second-year law student.

"*I think Jews are smarter than most people and I'm going to hang in there with my people. My political beliefs are clear and definite. We should never have been in Viet Nam. We have real problems at home. The blacks are pushing too hard. I think Secretary of State Kissinger has the real brains in this country.*

"*I dig chicks. I score a lot. If they want to give it, I'll take it. I got a girl pregnant once but she got an abortion. I think I'm lucky that it only happened once.*

"*I'm a go-getter. I'm not exactly on top in my class at law school but I'm going to make it big, get a job with a big company, get stock options, then go off on my own.*"

Physical description: Murray is tall, dark, and handsome. He dresses like an old-time matinee idol and speaks in a deep, rich voice.

Personal concern: Murray is pleasant and amusing. He wants to find out how to better himself as a leader and wonders why no one is following him. He makes heavy verbal attacks on people who disagree with him. He uses his fluency to take charge of most social situations. It is hard for him to stop talking.

WILL. White, male, age 30; B.S. and M.S. in biochemistry; employed as director of an experimental lab by a research and development firm; married, no children; wife employed.

"I'm not sure about religion. I don't think about it much. I have never been interested in politics. I play classical guitar and I hunt and fish. I like to be alone.

"My wife has recently been complaining about our marriage. I am not too interested in sex. I may have some homosexual tendencies but I don't see that as a problem—it's a choice I can make. I don't want any kids. My wife complains that we have few friends. I don't think we need more than two or three close friends."

Physical description: Will is 5 feet, 10 inches tall, weighs about 174 pounds. He has a neatly trimmed beard and moustache, dresses conservatively (somber suit, necktie), and projects a very neat and precise image.

Personal concern: Will is concerned about his "poor relations with others." He displays irritability in his dealings with women. His wife has complained about her inability to talk with him without incurring his anger. He says that he can dissociate from himself and watch himself behave, but when he "re-enters" himself, he becomes very angry with the people who happen to be around. He would like to learn the reasons behind his anger and some ways to control it. Right now he prefers to be with his superiors in the company, because their position prevents him from getting angry with them.

LEN. Black, male, age 45; high-school social-studies teacher; married, no children; member of the Protestant Episcopal Church.

"I still go to church, but it doesn't mean as much to me as it once did. I appreciate what some of the politicians have been trying to do for us, black and white alike, but some of them are opportunists. I try to teach my students to look at the man, as I do.

"I think my relationship with my wife is good. We have a good sexual relationship. She works hard to keep our home looking nice. I don't want her to work. I want to be the man in my house. I hope some day to go back to school to get a principal's credential. I surely don't want to teach in an inner-city school, though."

Physical description: Len is 6 feet tall, weighs about 200 pounds. He has a light brown complexion. His hair is closely cropped; he has a thin moustache and wears glasses. He dresses conservatively.

Personal concern: Len complains that he is lonely. He feels that his refusal to become involved in black political causes has cost him a lot of black friends. Most of his male friends have not married, and he feels that his marriage has also been an alienating force. He does not associate much with his colleagues because he is fearful that they see him only as a "token" black. He feels that his wife may be becoming bored with him, and he wants to learn how to cultivate relationships. Len says he is convinced that his "black experience" is as valid as those of blacks with a ghetto background. He reports that he feels "pretty satisfied—maybe too much so."

Structured Experience 172

IVAN. White, male, age 26; married, one child (boy, 6 months); owns and operates a farm near a large city.

"*I believe in the fellowship of the church and the sacred nature of the land. The farm is not doing too well, but as I get it changed over to truck-garden crops, it will do better. My wife cooks and cans a lot, and we are living an old-fashioned life. I think I would like to expand the farm so I can raise beef cattle in addition to the garden crops.*

"*A year ago, I had a brief affair and I feel pretty guilty about it. It happened only once, with a girl I didn't even know, and it has left me depressed and unhappy. Sometimes I get real suspicious, like someone is going to tell my wife about the affair. It would really break her heart if she knew.*"

Physical description: Ivan is over 6 feet tall and is well proportioned. He wears short hair and dresses in open-collar shirts and well-laundered jeans.

Personal concern: Ivan is worried about his daydreaming and sexual fantasies, and he feels that this is interfering with his relationship with his wife. He has become impotent since his affair a year ago. Ivan reports that he was always awkward with women and that his wife was the only woman he had ever dated. Ivan says that he feels he has missed out on a lot by not dating other women, and he is beginning to feel uneasy about his whole life style.

LOIS. White, female, age 37; married (to a stockbroker), two children; unemployed; graduate degree in social work.

"*I enjoyed working after graduation, but I began to worry about some of the parts of town I was working in and I couldn't handle some of the remarks—you know what I mean. I met my husband after I had been working one year and I loved him, so I just figured it was time to settle down.*

"*I am in a lot of activities. I am involved in the Junior League and I also work for a local day-care center. We live in a suburb; I go to most of the council meetings. I am running for Democratic committeewoman this year.*

"*My husband and I socialize a lot, mostly with people from his work or from the club. Most of them are older than we are but they are all potential customers. And we see our families a lot. They live close by.*"

Physical description: Lois is short and chunky. She has thick, long, black hair and looks more like a college freshman than a mother of two. She moves with considerable bounce; her voice is enthusiastic, though sometimes whiny.

Personal concern: Lois has been complaining of boredom. She has been reading a lot of women's lib literature and has been wondering lately if she was wise to give up her social-work job. She is most concerned about developing relationships with women her own age.

NANCY. White, female, age 26; librarian for the local medical center; currently working part time on an advanced library degree.

"I have a lot of conflict with my family. My parents are very concerned because I am not married. I am not interested in marriage. I have never been interested in men. There is nothing peculiar about me, I simply prefer the company of women. I have no sex life. I do not smoke or drink and have never used drugs. I have no deep political or religious commitments. I love art, music, and particularly theater, and I want the freedom to have as much of that as I like.

"I am not concerned about liberation propaganda but I do want the freedom to run my own life. Mostly, I want to be left alone. I have a few good friends and I am not terribly interested in meeting any more people."

Physical description: Nancy is of medium height and build and wears plain, almost austere clothing. She is not unattractive, but she studiously avoids accentuating any female characteristics in her dress.

Personal concern: Nancy wants help in dealing with males, particularly on her job. She feels that men are continually making "passes" at her. She takes elaborate precautions in her personal life, keeps a triple lock on her apartment door, and does not move about at night unless in the company of two or three other women. She wants to talk with someone about her fears.

ELLEN. White, female, age 19; liberal arts major at State University; has a B- average.

"I've been in a lot of demonstrations for people's rights. I enjoy the excitement and the feeling that I am doing something that matters.

"I easily become sexually excited and often find new and exciting partners. I've been on the pill since I was fifteen, but I don't think there is any evil in making love.

"I want to get a helping job where I can be of use to people in trouble and also have time to write poetry that describes my view of the world. I want to be free to be me and to love."

Physical description: Ellen is short, blonde, and somewhat heavy. She wears loose clothing and rarely wears shoes. Her clothing is usually covered with slogan-bearing buttons. Her hair is long and unkempt.

Personal concern: Friends have reported that Ellen has been excessively frank with them, revealing the most intimate details of her life in an unsolicited way. She tries to elicit the same information from others. She began to display these high-disclosure tendencies six months ago, after an encounter weekend sponsored by a local church. A roommate whom she respects has urged her to get into a group, but Ellen does not think she has a problem.

CONTRIBUTORS

Anthony G. Banet, Jr.
Senior Consultant
University Associates
7596 Eads Avenue
La Jolla, California 92037
(714) 454-8821

Geoff Bellman
Director of Development and Training
G. B. Searle & Company
P. O. Box 1045
Skokie, Illinois 60076
(312) 982-7666

Clarke G. Carney
Assistant Director
Counseling and Consultation Services
Student Services Building
The Ohio State University
154 W. 12th Avenue
Columbus, Ohio 43210
(614) 422-5766

Richard J. Carpenter, Jr.
Assistant Professor of Aerospace Studies
Wilkes College
Wilkes-Barre, Pennsylvania 18703
(717) 829-0194

J. Stephen Colladay
Career Counselor
Cornell College
Mt. Vernon, Iowa 52314
(319) 895-8811

Robert H. Dolliver
Associate Professor of Psychology
21 Stewart Hall
University of Missouri
Columbia, Missouri 65201
(314) 882-4255

Allan G. Dorn
Career Counselor
Arlington High School
502 West Euclid
Arlington Heights, Illinois 60005
(312) 253-0200

Philip M. Ericson
Assistant Professor
Speech and Theater Department
221 Administration
State University College
Oneonta, New York 13820
(607) 431-3402

Howard L. Fromkin
Associate Professor
Krannert Graduate School
   of Industrial Administration
Purdue University
West Lafayette, Indiana 47907

Frederick L. Goodman
Professor of Education
The University of Michigan
East and South University Avenues
Ann Arbor, Michigan 48104
(313) 764-1560

William V. Haney
President
William V. Haney Associates
2453 Cardinal Lane
Wilmette, Illinois 60091
(312) 251-5619

Brian P. Holleran
Assistant Professor
Speech and Theater Department
221 Administration
State University College
Oneonta, New York 13820
(607) 431-3402

John R. Joachim
Coordinator
Division of Enrichment Studies
Princeton City Schools
11157 Chester Road
Cincinnati, Ohio 45246
(513) 771-0780

John E. Jones
Vice-President
University Associates
7596 Eads Avenue
La Jolla, California 92037
(714) 454-8821

Colleen A. Kelley
Human Relations Consultant
4303 Mentone Street, #4
San Diego, California 92107
(714) 224-8911

Michael J. Miller
Director of Organizational Development
Independent Boxmakers, Inc.
515 Park Avenue
Louisville, Kentucky 40208
(502) 637-2574

Peter Mumford
Head, Staff Development and Training Unit
Department of Management and Business
  Studies
Brighton Polytechnic
Brighton, England

J. William Pfeiffer
President
University Associates
7596 Eads Avenue
La Jolla, California 92037
(714) 454-8821

Gerald M. Phillips
Professor of Speech Communication
Department of Speech
305 Sparks Building
Pennsylvania State University
University Park, Pennsylvania 16802
(814) 865-4072

Anthony J. Reilly
Senior Consultant
University Associates
7596 Eads Avenue
La Jolla, California 92037
(714) 454-8821

Peter R. Scholtes
Organizational Development Director
City of Madison
210 Monona Avenue
Madison, Wisconsin 53709
(608) 266-4790

Kenneth D. Scott
Institute of Industrial Relations
University of California
Berkeley, California 94720

John F. Veiga
Assistant Professor
Department of Industrial Administration
School of Business Administration
The University of Connecticut
Storrs, Connecticut 06268
(203) 486-3640

Allen A. Zoll III
Conferences and Publications
Management Education Associates
2208 White Henry Stuart Building
Seattle, Washington 98144
(206) 624-2205